MINNESOTA
TRIVIA

MINNESOTA TRIVIA

COMPILED BY LAUREL WINTER

Rutledge Hill Press
Nashville, Tennessee

Published by Rutledge Hill Press, Inc., 211 Seventh Avenue North, Nashville, Tennessee 37219.

Typography by Bailey Typography, Inc.
Cover by Linda Nelson

Printed in the United States of America
4 5 6 7 8 9—96 95 94

PREFACE

I ran out of space and time long before I ran out of Minnesota trivia. So, to those authors and actors and athletes and hometowns and festivals that I missed, please forgive me. This book would have been twice or thrice as long if it were "complete." And then some new stars of the North Star State would have appeared . . . .

The people of Minnesota kept turning up great tidbits. Like Tammy, who ended up giving us a private tour of the Metrodome, and Robert, security guard and actor who told me about Frank M. Whiting's *Minnesota Theatre: From Old Fort Snelling to the Guthrie*. The fabulous reference librarians at the Rochester Public Library, the archivists and alumni directors at Minnesota's colleges and universities, and the staff at the Minnesota Department of Tourism all helped, as well as many others.

I hope you enjoy this dip into the land of ten thousand lakes.

—Laurel Winter

To my husband, Bruce,
for the excellent help and motivation he provided
and to Terry Garey and Denny Lien

TABLE OF CONTENTS

Laurel Winter is a freelance writer. She is also *co-editor of* Blossoms and Blizzards, *an anthology of Minnesota authors.* She lives in Rochester, Minnesota.

GEOGRAPHY

CHAPTER ONE

Q. What Minnesota town is known as the "nation's ice-box"?

A. International Falls.

———◆———

Q. Where are the Minnesota Museum of Mining and Iron-world USA?

A. Chisholm.

———◆———

Q. In what town did Libby's build a water tower shaped like a corn cob?

A. Rochester.

———◆———

Q. What lake has more shoreline than any other in Minnesota?

A. Lake Vermilion (1,200 miles).

———◆———

Q. What was once known as Little Falls and Brown's Falls?

A. Minnehaha Falls.

Q. What outcropping of rock, once an island in the enlarged, postglacial Mississippi River, looms three hundred feet over the city of Red Wing?

A. Barn Bluff.

Q. Where is America's Steam Engine Capital?

A. Mabel.

Q. What is held in Sauk Centre in mid-July?

A. Sinclair Lewis Days.

Q. What is the self-proclaimed geographic center of Minnesota?

A. Chisholm.

Q. Where does the Minnesota Zephyr, a 1940s train with dining cars and Vista Dome club cars, travel from?

A. Stillwater.

Q. What is the Minnesota state muffin?

A. The blueberry muffin.

Q. What fraction of the distance from Hudson Bay to the Gulf of Mexico does Minnesota comprise?

A. More than one-fourth.

Q. What was the nation's first enclosed shopping mall, built in 1956?

A. Southdale (in Edina).

———◆———

Q. Where does Minnesota rank in percentage of homes with telephones?

A. Number one.

———◆———

Q. What town's annual festival involves the state mammal?

A. The Viola Gopher Count.

———◆———

Q. Where can you find one of the world's two aerial lift bridges?

A. Duluth.

———◆———

Q. Where can you find the August Schell Brewing Company, one of the nation's oldest family operated breweries?

A. New Ulm.

———◆———

Q. Where are the headwaters of the Mississippi?

A. Lake Itasca.

———◆———

Q. What is the average amount of time Twin Cities residents spend getting to work each day?

A. Twenty-three and one-half minutes.

Q. What does Minnesota have more of than California, Florida, and Hawaii combined?

A. Shoreline.

Q. How tall is the IDS tower, built in 1972?

A. Fifty-seven stories (775 feet).

Q. In how many states are St. Paul's Nut Goodies candy bars sold?

A. Only six.

Q. What family farm belonging to the founder of the Grange is now a living history farm southeast of Elk River on the banks of the Mississippi?

A. The Kelley farm.

Q. What is Minnesota's deepest lake?

A. Saganaga Lake (240 feet).

Q. Where is the Turtle Mound Trail?

A. Grand Rapids.

Q. What river got its name in 1864 because it had no bar at its mouth?

A. The Temperance River.

Q. What Minnesota festival is one of the nation's ten leading annual festivals?

A. The St. Paul Winter Carnival (started in 1886).

———◆———

Q. Where can one find a restored 1913 hotel that is accessible only by water?

A. Kettle Falls.

———◆———

Q. What two national monuments are in Minnesota?

A. Grand Portage National Monument and Pipestone National Monument.

———◆———

Q. In terms of area, how does Minnesota rank among the states?

A. Twelfth.

———◆———

Q. What did the Minnesota Historical Society re-create west of Pine City in 1960?

A. The North West Company Fur Post.

———◆———

Q. What town, founded in 1854 by members of the German Land Society, is named after a town in Wittenberg, Germany?

A. New Ulm.

———◆———

Q. What is the only four-year college or university in Minnesota with all academic and administrative buildings connected by skyways or tunnels?

A. Southwest State University (in Marshall).

Q. What city had an elevated monorail in 1888–89?

A. St. Paul.

———◆———

Q. What is the most northerly major tributary of the Mississippi River?

A. The Minnesota River.

———◆———

Q. Where does Minnesota rank in millionaires per capita among the fifty states?

A. Second.

———◆———

Q. How many state and federal campsites does Minnesota have?

A. Over six thousand.

———◆———

Q. What ethnically inspired nickname describes Minnesota?

A. Little Scandinavia.

———◆———

Q. Where was the last covered bridge in Minnesota?

A. Zumbrota (now part of a park).

———◆———

Q. How many miles of groomed snowmobile trails does Minnesota have?

A. Twelve thousand (more than any other state).

Q. What is the eighth windiest city in the United States?

A. Rochester.

———◆———

Q. In 1988, how many miles were driven by all drivers in Minnesota?

A. 36.4 billion.

———◆———

Q. When rich ore was discovered under it in 1918, what Minnesota town was relocated one mile south to Alice and then continued to move over the next forty years?

A. Hibbing.

———◆———

Q. What fraction of Minnesota's land is in public ownership?

A. Nearly one-fourth (about twelve million acres).

———◆———

Q. Where is the only stone arch bridge over the Mississippi River?

A. Below the Falls of St. Anthony.

———◆———

Q. What is known as Minnesota's "Grand Canyon"?

A. The Hull-Rust-Mahoning Mine.

———◆———

Q. Who disapproved of the second word in the name Superior Roadless Primitive Area?

A. Caterpillar Corporation.

Q. What three southeastern Minnesota counties were not covered by glaciers?

A. Houston, most of Filmore, and the south part of Winona.

Q. The M.A. Gedney Company, which has been making pickles since 1881, is in what Minnesota town?

A. Chaska.

Q. How did the Urban Institute of Washington, D.C., rank the Twin Cities for quality of life of all metropolitan areas in the United States?

A. Number one.

Q. Sauk Centre was given what name in Sinclair Lewis's *Main Street*?

A. Gopher Prairie.

Q. What town took the middle name of Minnesota's first governor?

A. Hastings (Henry Hastings Sibley).

Q. Where is Mrs. B's Historic Inn?

A. Lanesboro.

Q. What kind of facilities did approximately twelve out of thirteen Minnesota homes have in 1970?

A. Plumbing.

Q. What Minnesota town did John Wilson name for the city Napoleon built for the Empress Josephine?

A. St. Cloud.

———◆———

Q. How many miles does the Mississippi River travel from Lake Itasca to the Gulf of Mexico?

A. 2,552.

———◆———

Q. What is said to be the most beautiful lake in Minnesota, with 114 miles of shoreline?

A. Lake Minnetonka.

———◆———

Q. How many state parks are there in Minnesota?

A. Sixty-five.

———◆———

Q. What does Concordia College, Moorhead, hold in various states each fall?

A. Corn feeds.

———◆———

Q. How tall is the Sugar Loaf Monolith at Winona?

A. Five hundred feet above the Mississippi.

———◆———

Q. What was the largest prehistoric lake that once covered part of Minnesota?

A. Lake Agassiz.

Q. What town is called Red Leaf if its name is translated from the Sioux language?

A. Wabasha.

———◆———

Q. What proportion of Minnesota's population lives in the seven-county Minneapolis-St. Paul metro area?

A. One-half.

———◆———

Q. What was called Riviere St. Pierre by the French and St. Peter River by the British?

A. The Minnesota River.

———◆———

Q. What house in Mabel was ordered in pieces from a 1917 mail order catalog?

A. The Sears, Roebuck house.

———◆———

Q. What is the largest federal wilderness east of the Rockies?

A. The Boundary Waters Canoe Area (almost 1.1 million acres).

———◆———

Q. What Great Lakes ship is permanently docked near the Entertainment Convention Center in Duluth?

A. The *William A. Irvin*.

———◆———

Q. Where is the Mayo Clinic situated?

A. Rochester.

Q. What did Koo-poo-hoo-sha, meaning "wing of the wild swan dyed scarlet," become?

A. Red Wing.

———◆———

Q. What town unsuccessfully attempted a raid on Le Sueur in 1859, hoping to take county records but instead coming away with maps, some legal papers, and a desk?

A. Cleveland.

———◆———

Q. *Bemidji* is a Chippewa word with what meaning?

A. "Lake with river flowing through."

———◆———

Q. Where does the Mississippi River rank in size among the world's rivers?

A. Third largest.

———◆———

Q. How tall is Pigeon Falls, Minnesota's highest waterfall?

A. 130 feet.

———◆———

Q. While their numbers went down from 179,000 in 1950 to 99,000 in 1974, what increased in average size from 184 acres to 280 acres?

A. Minnesota's farms.

———◆———

Q. What Minnesota town has a fifteen-foot statue of a pelican, the largest in the world?

A. Pelican Rapids.

Q. What town has an annual Spanish festival in honor of its South American namesake?

A. Montevideo.

———◆———

Q. What is on the corner of Ninth and St. Peter streets in St. Paul?

A. Mickey's Diner.

———◆———

Q. What rural county grew 11.4 percent in the 1980s?

A. Roseau.

———◆———

Q. The Crabtree Kitchen Restaurant and an 1875 school are the only buildings in the location of what town once named Vasa for a Swedish king?

A. Otis.

———◆———

Q. Where can one tour caves dug in the 1880s to refrigerate food and preserve cadavers for the state hospital?

A. Quarry Hill Park (Rochester).

———◆———

Q. How many shopping malls were built in the seven-county metro area between 1984 and 1988?

A. Eighty.

———◆———

Q. The name *Minneapolis* comes from what two languages?

A. Sioux (*minne* means "water") and Greek (*polis* means "city").

Q. What town contains the plaque celebrating the Minnesota Territorial Convention?

A. Stillwater.

———◆———

Q. Where did Deborah Anderson found the nation's second rape crisis center in 1973?

A. Minneapolis.

———◆———

Q. With 13.8 percent of Minnesota males being college graduates in 1970, what percentage of Minnesota females were college graduates?

A. 8.6 percent.

———◆———

Q. Where is the International Elks Curling Bonspiel held?

A. Duluth.

———◆———

Q. In what direction does the Red River of the North flow?

A. North.

———◆———

Q. What town began a pottery industry after fine clay was found there?

A. Red Wing.

———◆———

Q. What do Lancaster, Malung, and Mora all have?

A. Sister cities in Sweden that share their town names.

Q. Who are the royalty at the St. Paul Winter Carnival?

A. King Boreas and the Queen of the Snows.

━━━━◆━━━━

Q. How far has the edge of St. Anthony Falls moved back in historic times, because of the soft stone underpinning?

A. About four blocks.

━━━━◆━━━━

Q. Where is the birthplace of the snowmobile and the home of Polaris Industries?

A. Roseau.

━━━━◆━━━━

Q. How many acres are in the sixty-five Minnesota state parks?

A. About 160,000 acres.

━━━━◆━━━━

Q. How large is the IBM building in Rochester?

A. 3.5 million square feet (the largest IBM under one contiguous roof in the world).

━━━━◆━━━━

Q. Where can one find Upper Town, with southern residents; Middle Town, with easterners; and Lower Town, with German residents?

A. St. Cloud.

━━━━◆━━━━

Q. What does the twenty-eight-foot granite spire memorial in the Moose Lake cemetery commemorate?

A. The 453 people killed in the 1918 fire.

Q. Minnesota is one of only how many states between the urban east and the Rocky Mountains that is above the national average in educational achievement?

A. Three.

———◆———

Q. How many counties in Minnesota do not have hospitals?

A. Four.

———◆———

Q. What is held in Northfield the weekend after Labor Day?

A. Defeat of Jesse James Days.

———◆———

Q. What was Two Harbors originally called?

A. Agate Bay.

———◆———

Q. Where is the northernmost navigable point of the Mississippi River?

A. St. Anthony Falls.

———◆———

Q. To what body of salt water is Minnesota closest?

A. Hudson Bay.

———◆———

Q. Where is the Midwest's only university design and fashion museum?

A. University of Minnesota St. Paul campus (the Goldstein Gallery).

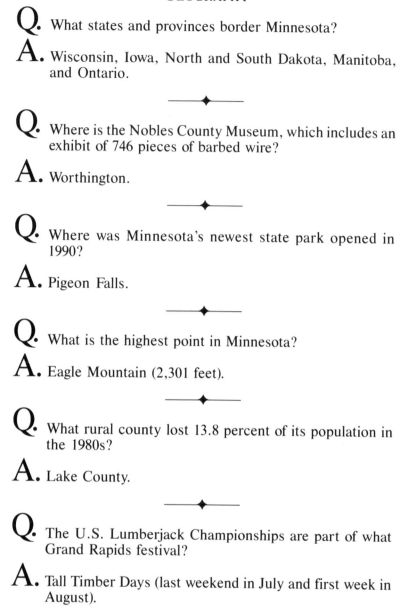

Q. What states and provinces border Minnesota?

A. Wisconsin, Iowa, North and South Dakota, Manitoba, and Ontario.

———◆———

Q. Where is the Nobles County Museum, which includes an exhibit of 746 pieces of barbed wire?

A. Worthington.

———◆———

Q. Where was Minnesota's newest state park opened in 1990?

A. Pigeon Falls.

———◆———

Q. What is the highest point in Minnesota?

A. Eagle Mountain (2,301 feet).

———◆———

Q. What rural county lost 13.8 percent of its population in the 1980s?

A. Lake County.

———◆———

Q. The U.S. Lumberjack Championships are part of what Grand Rapids festival?

A. Tall Timber Days (last weekend in July and first week in August).

———◆———

Q. What two paddlewheel steamboats dock at Wabasha?

A. The *Delta Queen* and *Mississippi Queen*.

Q. What is Minnesota's northernmost point, also the northernmost point in the forty-eight contiguous states?

A. The Northwest Angle (jutting into Lake of the Woods).

———◆———

Q. What southeastern Minnesota city has been restored to its original 1880s appearance?

A. Mantorville.

———◆———

Q. What country is Minnesota's leading export market?

A. Canada.

———◆———

Q. What is the largest island in the Mississippi River?

A. Prairie Island (south of Hastings).

———◆———

Q. What was the Twin Cities' metropolitan area population in 1984?

A. 2,231,000.

———◆———

Q. Where is the Steamboat Museum?

A. Winona.

———◆———

Q. Where in Minnesota is there a replica of an 1870s lumbertown?

A. Gull Lake (Lumbertown USA).

Q. When did St. Cloud incorporate its three separate towns into one?

A. 1856.

———◆———

Q. Where is the restored Sibley House next door to Faribault House?

A. Mendota.

———◆———

Q. By what nickname is the Mississippi River known?

A. "The Father of Waters."

———◆———

Q. What does Hiawathaland claim to have more of per person than anywhere else in the United States?

A. Antique shops.

———◆———

Q. Where is the only Civil War recruiting station left in Minnesota?

A. Wasioja.

———◆———

Q. What town was an important stage relay station between St. Paul and Superior, Wisconsin?

A. Hinckley.

———◆———

Q. What is held at Leech Lake in mid-February?

A. The annual Eelpout Festival.

Q. Where is the world's largest freshwater port?

A. Duluth.

———◆———

Q. In 1860, the population of New Ulm included how many Germans who retained their native language and customs?

A. 653.

———◆———

Q. How many islands does the Lake of the Woods contain?

A. Fourteen thousand.

———◆———

Q. Hastings, with sixty buildings of historical significance, is one of five Minnesota towns with what designation?

A. "Main Street" towns.

———◆———

Q. At what college is the annual Swayed Pines Folk Festival held?

A. St. John's University (Collegeville).

———◆———

Q. Where is Minnesota's oldest operating hotel?

A. Wabasha (the Anderson House).

———◆———

Q. What is the largest Lutheran seminary in the western hemisphere?

A. Luther Northwestern Theological Seminary in St. Paul.

Q. Where is the Aquatennial held?

A. Minneapolis.

✦

Q. What is the "City in a Rock Garden"?

A. Duluth.

✦

Q. The German celebration *Fasching*, which includes a masquerade ball, is held the weekend before Ash Wednesday in what city?

A. New Ulm.

✦

Q. What event boasts a massive ice castle?

A. The St. Paul Winter Carnival.

✦

Q. Where are the Paul Bunyan Center and the Croft Mine Historical Park?

A. Brainerd.

✦

Q. What did Cuyler Adams name after himself and his dog?

A. The Cuyuna Range.

✦

Q. Climatically, the Twin Cities and Duluth resemble what international capital?

A. Moscow.

Q. What was the first graduate school of medicine, established in 1915?

A. The Mayo Graduate School of Medicine (Rochester).

———◆———

Q. Where are King Korn Days held in mid-September?

A. Fairmont.

———◆———

Q. What urban county grew 23.3 percent in the 1980s?

A. Dakota.

———◆———

Q. What is now a trading post for an Ojibway reservation north of the Rum River?

A. Vineland.

———◆———

Q. Where is the valley of the Jolly Green Giant?

A. The Minnesota River Valley (LeSueur).

———◆———

Q. How long ago was the Soudan Iron Formation created?

A. 2.6 to 2.7 billion years.

———◆———

Q. What is the westernmost source of the St. Lawrence River?

A. The St. Louis River, which empties into Lake Superior at Duluth.

Q. What city was known as the "wickedest city in the world" in the late 1800s?

A. Moorhead.

◆

Q. What event is held in Pipestone the last two weekends in July and the first weekend in August?

A. The Song of Hiawatha Pageant.

◆

Q. What recently created national park lies near International Falls?

A. Voyageurs National Park.

◆

Q. Where is the Village of Yesteryear?

A. Owatonna.

◆

Q. What percentage of Minnesota's population consisted of minorities in 1989?

A. Four percent.

◆

Q. Where is the Korn and Klover Karnival held during two days in mid-August?

A. Hinckley.

◆

Q. How many counties are there in Minnesota?

A. Eighty-seven.

Q. What three parks were donated to the city of St. Paul in 1849, before Central Park was established in New York?

A. Irvine, Rice, and Smith parks.

———◆———

Q. What city was named for the narrows created in a lake by a sand bar?

A. Detroit Lakes.

———◆———

Q. How long is the St. Croix National Scenic Riverway?

A. Two hundred miles.

———◆———

Q. What city was destroyed twice by fires, in 1893 and 1900?

A. Virginia.

———◆———

Q. What is the source of the Minnesota River, the only river to run its entire length in the state that bears its name?

A. Big Stone Lake.

———◆———

Q. Fergus Falls was named for James Fergus, who lent what to founder James Whitfield in 1857?

A. A dog team.

———◆———

Q. What city is the largest river port in the upper Midwest?

A. St. Paul.

Q. What college ranks fourth among the nation's liberal arts colleges in the number of students who become Rhodes scholars?

A. Macalester.

———◆———

Q. What Minnesota county extends farthest east?

A. Cook.

———◆———

Q. What state property contains the second highest point in Minnesota?

A. Inspiration Peak State Wayside, near Urbank (1,750 feet).

———◆———

Q. What is Minnesota's largest county, bigger than the state of Connecticut?

A. St. Louis.

———◆———

Q. What Minnesota city was one of ten in the nation to be named an All America City in 1988?

A. Rochester.

———◆———

Q. What did Proctor Knott refer to as the "zenith city of the unsalted seas"?

A. Duluth.

———◆———

Q. How large is Voyageurs National Park?

A. 219,000 acres (land and water).

Q. Hastings is situated at the convergence of what three rivers?

A. The Mississippi, St. Croix, and Vermillion.

———◆———

Q. Minnesota's Northwest Angle, which is separated from the rest of the state by the Lake of the Woods, is physically attached to what Canadian province?

A. Manitoba.

———◆———

Q. Where is the Freeze Yer Gizzard Blizzard Run held?

A. International Falls (part of Ice Box Days).

———◆———

Q. Where is the Father Hennepin Stone?

A. Anoka (near the mouth of the Rum River).

———◆———

Q. What is Minnesota's smallest county, thirty-nine times smaller than St. Louis County, the largest?

A. Ramsey County.

———◆———

Q. What lake, thirteenth largest in Minnesota, is named for an Indian princess believed to be buried in one of the mounds bordering the lake's northern shore?

A. Lake Minnewaska.

———◆———

Q. Where can visitors cross the Mississippi River on stepping stones?

A. Itasca State Park.

Q. What was the last county established in Minnesota?

A. Lake of the Woods (1922).

———◆———

Q. What river separates Moorhead from Fargo, North Dakota?

A. The Red River of the North.

———◆———

Q. Where are King Turkey Days and the Great Gobbler Gallop held in September?

A. Worthington.

———◆———

Q. What does *Mesabi* mean?

A. "Giant."

———◆———

Q. A nonoperational mill can be found at Phelps Mill Park on what river?

A. Otter Tail River.

———◆———

Q. What is the only city of its size with two colleges that are both frequently listed among the nation's top ten small colleges?

A. Northfield (Carlton and St. Olaf).

———◆———

Q. What is nicknamed Minnesota's "air-conditioned city"?

A. Duluth.

Q. What house in Homer is an example of 1850s Steamboat Gothic architecture?

A. The Bunnell House.

———————◆———————

Q. What Algonquian Indian word means "Great River"?

A. *Mississippi.*

———————◆———————

Q. What did Piquadinaw become?

A. Quadna.

———————◆———————

Q. Bethel was first settled by what religious group?

A. Quakers.

———————◆———————

Q. How many Minnesota cities had populations over 40,000 in 1988?

A. Twelve.

———————◆———————

Q. What township was named after the Sioux Indian words meaning "sugar maple"?

A. Chanhassen.

———————◆———————

Q. What city had the names *All Saints, Hennepin, Lowell, Brooklyn,* and *Albion*?

A. Minneapolis.

Q. What is Duluth's renovated 1892 railroad station called?

A. The Depot.

———◆———

Q. Although there are none in Minnesota's seven northeastern counties, what covers 37 percent of Faribault County?

A. Soybeans.

———◆———

Q. What is the elevation at St. Paul?

A. 687 feet.

———◆———

Q. In 1977 what covered 27 percent of Minnesota's land?

A. Commercial forests.

———◆———

Q. Wasioja takes its name from the Sioux name for what river?

A. The Zumbro.

———◆———

Q. What city was named for a young Dakota woman who threw herself to her death from Maiden Rock?

A. Winona.

———◆———

Q. What festival that celebrates Minnesota's other "state bird" is held at the Forest History Center near Grand Rapids?

A. Mosquito Day.

Q. What state park spans both sides of the St. Croix River?

A. Interstate State Park.

———◆———

Q. What town is the birthplace of the ice cream sandwich?

A. Blue Earth.

———◆———

Q. *Minnetonka* means what?

A. "Big Water."

———◆———

Q. In the early twentieth century, what was the only big amusement park to be found between Chicago and the West Coast?

A. Wonderland (built by H.A. Donnelly).

———◆———

Q. What lake takes its name from the Latin words *veritas* and *caput*?

A. Itasca (subtract the first and last three letters).

———◆———

Q. What does *Lac Qui Parle* mean in French?

A. "Lake that talks."

———◆———

Q. According to a 1978 survey, what percentage of Minnesota households vacationed in the state?

A. About 31 percent.

Q. What county takes its name from the Ojibway Indian word meaning "wild rice"?

A. Mahnomen.

———◆———

Q. What comprises 90 percent of nine western, southwestern, and southern counties but only .1 percent of Cook County?

A. Farms.

———◆———

Q. What does the town of New York Mills straddle?

A. A continental divide.

———◆———

Q. What other state has both a Minneapolis and a St. Paul?

A. Kansas.

———◆———

Q. What are Vikingland, Heartland, Arrowhead, Metroland, Pioneerland, and Hiawathaland?

A. Minnesota's six tourism regions.

———◆———

Q. What county seat was first called Montezuma?

A. Winona.

———◆———

Q. How many official lakes does Minnesota have?

A. 15,291.

ENTERTAINMENT

C H A P T E R   T W O

Q. What movie, based on a Kurt Vonnegut novel, was filmed in Minneapolis and directed by George Roy Hill?

A. *Slaughterhouse Five.*

——◆——

Q. What is Valleyfair's biggest new roller coaster?

A. Excalibur.

——◆——

Q. What St. Thomas graduate has appeared on "Bronx Zoo," "You Are the Jury," and "Highway to Heaven"?

A. Patrick O'Bryan.

——◆——

Q. What family does the community pageant *Fragments of a Dream* portray?

A. The Ingalls family (Walnut Grove).

——◆——

Q. What was the first full-time professional chamber orchestra established in the United States?

A. The St. Paul Chamber Orchestra (then the St. Paul Philharmonic).

Q. What Plymouth-based record company sells records primarily over television?

A. K-Tel.

――――◆――――

Q. What is the longest-running festival on the same theme in the world?

A. The St. Olaf Christmas Festival (started in 1912).

――――◆――――

Q. Who manipulated the glove puppets Towser the Dog and Tallulah the Cat on WCCO's "Axel and His Dog"?

A. Don Stolz.

――――◆――――

Q. What group, founded in 1980, swept the Minnesota Music Awards in 1987?

A. The Wallets.

――――◆――――

Q. What is the oldest continuously operating theater in the United States?

A. The Old Log Theatre.

――――◆――――

Q. Where are the ruby slippers and Dorothy's blue gingham dress from *The Wizard of Oz*?

A. Grand Rapids.

――――◆――――

Q. What Polynesian family band comes from Maple Grove?

A. The Jets.

Q. What *On Golden Pond* actor attended the University of Minnesota?

A. Henry Fonda.

———◆———

Q. Where is comedian Scott Novotne from?

A. Rochester.

———◆———

Q. What is Machine No. 33, made by the Philadelphia Toboggan Company in 1914?

A. The Minnesota State Fair carousel.

———◆———

Q. What Minnesota guitarist recorded "Greenhouse"?

A. Leo Kottke.

———◆———

Q. Where did hair stylist Rocco Altobelli grow up?

A. Dilworth.

———◆———

Q. What animated brand symbol celebrated his twenty-fifth birthday in Minneapolis in 1990?

A. The Pillsbury Doughboy?

———◆———

Q. In what unusual theater did Loni Anderson act before starring in "WKRP in Cincinnati"?

A. The Minnesota Centennial Showboat.

Q. What Medicine Lake native—the only American in Monty Python's Flying Circus—directed *Brazil*?

A. Terry Gilliam.

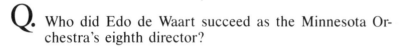

Q. Who did Edo de Waart succeed as the Minnesota Orchestra's eighth director?

A. Neville Marriner.

Q. What radio talk-show host was once Wrangler Steve on WCCO?

A. Steve Cannon.

Q. What is the meaning of *Penumbra*, the name of St. Paul's black professional theater?

A. "Half-shadow."

Q. How many Top 40 hits were produced by Minnesota studios or performed by Minnesota artists in the 1980s?

A. Forty-two.

Q. Where in Minnesota are jousting knights and wandering minstrels found during August and September?

A. The Renaissance Festival in Shakopee.

Q. What University of Minnesota debate coach later became a U.S. senator from Oregon?

A. Wayne Morse.

Q. What was the original name of The Replacements?

A. The Impediments.

———◆———

Q. Who starred in the Iron Range movie *Wildrose*?

A. Lisa Eichhorn and Tom Bower.

———◆———

Q. Who is the only bassoonist in the Fargo–Moorhead Orchestra?

A. Peter Schickele (P.D.Q. Bach).

———◆———

Q. What is Prince's ten-million-dollar multimedia studio in Chanhassen called?

A. Paisley Park.

———◆———

Q. What "Mission Impossible" star was born in Minneapolis in 1926?

A. Peter Graves.

———◆———

Q. What kiddie show character did Clellan Card play?

A. Axel the Carpenter.

———◆———

Q. What group recorded "Old Time" and "Live on Radio"?

A. LeRoy Larson and the Minnesota Scandinavian Ensemble.

Q. What five-foot, three-inch Anoka resident became Miss America in 1989?

A. Gretchen Carlson.

———◆———

Q. What was the only North American choral group chosen to participate in the World Symposium on Choral Music?

A. The Dale Warland Singers.

———◆———

Q. What August Wilson play released on Broadway in 1987 won a Tony Award?

A. *Fences.*

———◆———

Q. What Guinness world record did Beth Obermeyer orchestrate for the Hennepin Center of the Arts's grand opening in 1979?

A. The world's largest tap-dance line (1,801 dancers along Hennepin Avenue).

———◆———

Q. Where was actress Linda Kelsey born?

A. The Twin Cities.

———◆———

Q. What is known as the "Cadillac of Dinner Theatres"?

A. The Chanhassen Dinner Theatre.

———◆———

Q. Where was polka legend Whoopee John born?

A. New Ulm.

Q. What star of "The Lawyers" was from Owatonna?

A. E.G. Marshall.

———◆———

Q. What title was Barbara Peterson Burwell awarded in 1976?

A. Miss U.S.A.

———◆———

Q. What 1990 TV movie was shot in Minneapolis?

A. *Voices Within: The Lives of Truddi Chase.*

———◆———

Q. What Prince alter ego is created by speeding up the singer's voice?

A. Camille.

———◆———

Q. What did the Powderhorn Puppet Theatre become?

A. In the Heart of the Beast Puppet and Mask Theatre.

———◆———

Q. Sauk Centre was one of how many small towns Jessica Lange lived in as a child?

A. Eighteen.

———◆———

Q. What ABC sitcom starring Craig T. Nelson is set in Minneapolis?

A. "Coach."

Q. What did St. Olaf graduate Nancy Ringham star in opposite Rex Harrison in 1981 when the lead developed laryngitis?

A. The Broadway revival of *My Fair Lady*.

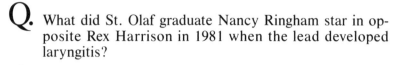

Q. What radio partner of Charlie Boone once played Bozo the Clown and had a show called "Rrrroger!" in 1964?

A. Roger Erickson.

Q. How old did Lyceum Theatre manager and director—and sometime actor—Dick Ferris purport to be from 1905 until his death in 1933?

A. Thirty-eight.

Q. Who recorded Janet Jackson's "Rhythm Nation" and "Control"?

A. Flyte Tyme Production (South Minneapolis and Edina).

Q. Where was Loni Anderson born?

A. St. Paul.

Q. What Brooklyn Park professional wrestler became a movie actor?

A. Jesse ("The Body") Ventura.

Q. What integrated theater, based in an 1887 firehouse, emphasizes colorblind casting?

A. The Mixed Blood Theatre.

Q. What did Don Powell, Stevie Wonder's former manager, change the group Quasar's name to?

A. The Jets.

———◆———

Q. What politician's daughter became a reporter for WCCO-TV in Minneapolis?

A. Eleanor Mondale.

———◆———

Q. Who met his future wife, Ann Martell, a student at Gustavus Adolphus, while on tour as a member of the Chad Mitchell Trio in 1966?

A. John Denver.

———◆———

Q. What media personality played Clancy the Keystone Cop and Commodore Cappy?

A. John Gallos.

———◆———

Q. Where was Jane Russell born?

A. Bemidji.

———◆———

Q. What does GNAT stand for?

A. The Great North American History Theatre.

———◆———

Q. What Minnesotan was Miss America in 1948?

A. BeBe Shopp Waring.

Q. No seat is more than how many rows away from center stage of the Theatre in the Round Players?

A. Seven.

---◆---

Q. What star of *The Birds* was born in Lafayette?

A. Tippi Hedren.

---◆---

Q. What group's writers had five plays on Broadway in 1988?

A. The Playwrights' Center (*Fences* and *Joe Turner's Come and Gone* by August Wilson, *The Gospel at Colonus* by Lee Breuer, *A Walk in the Woods* by Lee Blessing, and *The Dead* by Matthew Witten.)

---◆---

Q. What married couple hosts "Good Company"?

A. Steve Edelman and Sharon Anderson.

---◆---

Q. What Minnesota singer recorded the soundtrack for the movie *Batman*?

A. Prince.

---◆---

Q. What program, produced by KTCA-TV, focuses on new works in theater, dance, and performance art?

A. "Alive from Off Center."

---◆---

Q. What comedian wrote the very serious *Dear Dad*?

A. Louie Anderson.

Q. What "My Three Sons" cast member was born in St. Paul?

A. William Demarest.

———◆———

Q. Where is the only place Buddy Guy will play in the Twin Cities?

A. The Blues Saloon.

———◆———

Q. What theatrical couple became mayor and first lady of Minneapolis in 1933?

A. Buzz and Mary Gale Bainbridge.

———◆———

Q. What co-host of a daytime WCCO talk show became the national sales director of a cosmetic company?

A. Shirley Hutton (Mary Kay).

———◆———

Q. What St. Paul native was Billie Newman on "The Lou Grant Show"?

A. Linda Kelsey.

———◆———

Q. What was formerly known as *The General John Newton*?

A. The Minnesota Centennial Showboat.

———◆———

Q. What group had the top ten dance hit "What's on Your Mind?" after moving from Minneapolis to New York?

A. Information Society (1988).

Q. What "MacGyver" star was born in Minneapolis?

A. Richard Dean Anderson.

———◆———

Q. What Minnesotan recorded "YM"?

A. Steve Tibbets.

———◆———

Q. What was the first movie shown in Minnesota, in 1898, by longtime theatre manager Theodore Hays?

A. *The Great Train Robbery.*

———◆———

Q. What theater group developed *Touch* for children and *No Easy Answers* for adolescents?

A. The Illusion Theater.

———◆———

Q. What group played their first gig at St. Paul's Randolph Inn in 1979?

A. Hüsker Dü.

———◆———

Q. How old was Bob Dylan when he gave his first performance in his father's office, singing into a Dictaphone?

A. Three years old.

———◆———

Q. What Minnesota actor played in *The Vanishing American* and *The Quarterback?*

A. Richard Dix.

Q. What group was chosen in national competition to represent America in Monaco at the International Festival of Community Theatres?

A. The Theatre in the Round Players (TRP).

———◆———

Q. What comedian once played as soloist with the Minneapolis Symphony Orchestra?

A. Jack Benny (on his violin).

———◆———

Q. Who was the most famous employee of station WJM?

A. Mary Richards (Mary Tyler Moore).

———◆———

Q. What all-star group does Marian Moore promote?

A. Women Who Cook.

———◆———

Q. Where does Minneapolis's Theatre de la Jeune Lune spend half of its time?

A. Paris, France.

———◆———

Q. What Minneapolis-born actress starred in *My Wild Irish Rose*, *Three Little Words*, and *Inside Straight*?

A. Arlene Dahl.

———◆———

Q. What was Bob Dylan's first band as a teenager in Hibbing?

A. The Golden Chords.

Q. What "Happy Days" cast member was from Albert Lea?

A. Marion Ross.

———◆———

Q. What did Duddley Riggs establish at Seven Corners in Minneapolis?

A. The ETC (Experimental Theatre Company).

———◆———

Q. What Will Weaver novel was released as a television movie in 1989?

A. *Red Earth, White Earth.*

———◆———

Q. What was Dave Lee's sidekick on the KMSP children's show "Popeye and Pete"?

A. A penguin-puppet who was fond of pulling little girls' hair.

———◆———

Q. What song by The Lipps, Inc., was the number one dance single produced in the Twin Cities in 1980?

A. "Funkytown."

———◆———

Q. Grand Rapids-born Frances Gumm was better known by what name?

A. Judy Garland.

———◆———

Q. Who selected the University Theatre to tour France and Germany with *A Midsummer Night's Dream* in 1957?

A. The Department of Defense.

Q. Mary Tyler Moore, Donald Sutherland, and Timothy Hutton starred in what movie based on the Judith Guest novel?

A. *Ordinary People.*

◆

Q. What "Newhart" actress was born in the Twin Cities?

A. Julia Duffy.

◆

Q. What was the name of Garrison Keillor's popular radio show broadcast from the Twin Cities?

A. "A Prairie Home Companion."

◆

Q. Where did Jessica Lange attend high school?

A. Cloquet.

◆

Q. What former St. Paul boxer became an actor and also appeared in Baker's Square commercials?

A. Jim Beattie.

◆

Q. Who was the star of the kids' talent show "Jimmy's Junior Jamboree"?

A. Jimmy Valentine.

◆

Q. What show did Bob Dylan refuse to perform on when he was banned from singing "Talkin' John Birch Society Blues"?

A. The Ed Sullivan Show.

Q. Carol Bly and Judith Guest collaborated on what film set in Minnesota?

A. *Rachel River* (1988).

✦

Q. Where was Winona Ryder, who starred in the movie *Beetlejuice,* born?

A. Winona.

✦

Q. What group was first known as Loud Fast Rules?

A. Soul Asylum.

✦

Q. What actor, a member of the Shubert Players in 1917, became a film gangster and was featured in the "Mr. President" series on radio?

A. Eddie Albert.

✦

Q. What Maplewood comic prepared "What's So Funny about Being Female"?

A. Susan Vass.

✦

Q. What *Back to the Future* star was born in Minneapolis?

A. Lea Thompson.

✦

Q. Minneapolis natives Ed Flanders and Karen Landry were cast members for what television show?

A. "St. Elsewhere."

Q. What was the Twin Cities' first playhouse, built by Henry Van Liew in 1857?

A. The People's Theatre.

———◆———

Q. Robert Moulton of the University of Minnesota was asked to choreograph "The Grassland Suite" for whose visit to Canada?

A. Queen Elizabeth.

———◆———

Q. Who appeared as the mysterious masked folksinger on "A Prairie Home Companion"?

A. Jon Pankake.

———◆———

Q. What group did jazz choreographer Danny Buraczeski begin in Minnesota?

A. Zenon Dance Company.

———◆———

Q. What group recorded the album "From the Ladle to the Grave" on Willie Murphy's Atomic Theory label?

A. Boiled in Lead.

———◆———

Q. Who plays Minneapolis TV news anchor Christine Armstrong on "Coach"?

A. Shelley Fabares.

———◆———

Q. How many fans listened to the Beatles in their 1965 concert at the Met?

A. Only 30,000.

Q. How many one-hour shows did Roger Awsumb host daily as Casey?

A. Three ("Wake Up with Casey and Roundhouse," "Lunch with Casey," and "Casey and Roundhouse at Grandma Lumpit's Boarding House").

◆

Q. Who is the host of "Twin Cities Live"?

A. Bob Bruce.

◆

Q. What is Prince's full name?

A. Prince Rogers Nelson.

◆

Q. Who starred in the 1957 movie about Minnesota's famous outlaw, *The True Story of Jesse James*?

A. Robert Wagner and Hope Lange.

◆

Q. What Minnesota-born engineer inspired a folk song?

A. Casey Jones.

◆

Q. What Twin Cities group has recorded with Fine Young Cannibals?

A. The Steele Siblings.

◆

Q. Where were William Gibson's *A Cry of Players* and Robert Penn Warren's *All the King's Men* first presented?

A. The University Theatre, in Minneapolis.

Q. What all-female power-guitar band has Imaginary Records as its own label?

A. The Clams.

Q. On a visit to what place did Antonin Dvořak write notes for *Opus 100, the Indian Maiden*?

A. Minnehaha Falls.

Q. What star of *All Quiet on the Western Front* was born in Minneapolis in 1908?

A. Lew Ayres.

Q. What group was named the best local band with local portfolio in the February 1990 *Mpls–St. Paul Magazine*?

A. The Magnolias.

Q. What was Jimmy Valentine's stump-the-host show called?

A. "Riddle Griddle."

Q. What do more women aged eighteen to fifty turn to than all other Twin Cities' television stations combined at 3:00 P.M.?

A. KSTP (for "Good Company").

Q. What members of the band Time became record producers?

A. Jimmy Jam Harris and Terry Lewis.

Q. What was the motorized stage lift in the Eastside Players' old German–Presbyterian church originally designed to lift?

A. Coffins (the church was used as a mortuary earlier).

———◆———

Q. What Twin Cities' extracurricular theatre group celebrated its seventy-fifth anniversary in 1988?

A. The Punchinello Players (University of Minnesota St. Paul campus).

———◆———

Q. What Minnesota product inspired the first singing radio commercial?

A. Wheaties.

———◆———

Q. On what independent record label does Bob Feldman produce the work of Claudia Schmidt, Greg Brown, and the Mando Boys?

A. Red House Records.

———◆———

Q. What character did Lynn Duyer portray in the "Casey" shows?

A. Roundhouse Rodney.

———◆———

Q. What six-foot, seven-inch television star was born in Minneapolis in 1923?

A. James Arness.

———◆———

Q. Who won a Grammy for producers of the year in 1986?

A. Flyte Tyme Production (Janet Jackson's "Control").

Q. A scene from *Rip Van Winkle,* put on by the Minnesota Centennial Showboat company in 1962, was included in what one-hour television special?

A. Jacqueline Kennedy's "A Stage for Excellence."

———◆———

Q. Who did Robert Zimmerman, born in Duluth in 1941, become?

A. Bob Dylan.

———◆———

Q. From where was the third annual "Land O'Loons Comedy Special" broadcast?

A. The new Minnesota Telecenter.

———◆———

Q. "Saturday Night Live" performers Al Franken and Tom Davis came from what Minnesota city?

A. St. Louis Park.

———◆———

Q. Who collaborated with Willie Murphy on *Running, Jumping, Standing Still* (1969)?

A. John Koerner.

———◆———

Q. What is the oldest community theatre in the United States?

A. The Duluth Playhouse.

———◆———

Q. What instrument do the Mando Boys play?

A. Mandolins.

Q. What play did St. Cloud University present in China when it was selected in 1987 to tour in mainland China?

A. *The Wizard of Oz.*

———◆———

Q. What sport did Prince play at Central High in Minneapolis?

A. Basketball.

———◆———

Q. What did Lew Ayres do during World War II that hurt his career?

A. Declared himself a conscientious objector.

———◆———

Q. What Minnesota college broadcast the first radio drama in U.S. history in 1924?

A. St. Olaf *(As You Like It).*

———◆———

Q. What was Minnesota's first punk band to record on a national label?

A. The Suicide Commandos (1978, Mercury Records).

———◆———

Q. What actor, who first showed his frightening screen persona as Tommy Udo in *Kiss of Death* (1947), is from Sunrise, Minnesota?

A. Richard Widmark.

———◆———

Q. *Dear Digby,* the first novel of St. Paul native Carol Muske-Dukes, has been optioned by what actress?

A. Michelle Pfeiffer.

Q. In what movie did eleven-year-old Minnesotan Charlie Korsmo star?

A. *Dick Tracy.*

———◆———

Q. What was the Castaways' 1965 hit single?

A. "Liar, Liar."

———◆———

Q. What group, originating in Minneapolis, was forbidden by their manager to take singing lessons after selling eight million records?

A. The Andrews Sisters.

———◆———

Q. What was the former occupation of comedian Louie Anderson?

A. Social worker.

———◆———

Q. By what name is Waconia native Don Herbert better known?

A. "Mr. Wizard."

———◆———

Q. What 1958 Disney featurette was set in Minnesota?

A. *Paul Bunyan.*

———◆———

Q. Who produces Gladys Knight & the Pips, New Edition, Human League, and George Michael?

A. Flyte Tyme Production.

Q. What jazz artist taught music at the University of Minnesota for twenty years before dying during heart surgery in 1988?

A. Reginald Buckner.

---◆---

Q. What did Rochester-born comedian David Wood open in 1985?

A. David Wood's Rib Tickler Comedy and Magic Club.

---◆---

Q. Who was the first actress to receive a double Oscar nomination since 1942?

A. Jessica Lange.

---◆---

Q. What two movies dealing with Minnesota's pioneer days were released in 1971 and 1972?

A. *The Emigrants* and *The New Land*.

---◆---

Q. Who is the Lamont Cranston band named after?

A. A secret identity of The Shadow.

---◆---

Q. What Showboat actress went on to leading roles in such Broadway productions as *Stop the World, I Want to Get Off* and *Oliver* before dying at age thirty-two?

A. Joan Eastman.

---◆---

Q. Where did Shipstad and Johnson's Ice Follies originate?

A. The Twin Cities.

Q. What Flyte Tyme lead singer went gold in the United States with *Hearsay,* an album that includes the Top 40 single "Fake"?

A. Alexander O'Neal.

———◆———

Q. In what movie did young Mark Vande Brake from Granite Falls play a dwarf child?

A. *Willow.*

———◆———

Q. What was Bob Dylan's original stage name?

A. Bob Dillon.

———◆———

Q. Who is the main comic character in Charles Lindholm's one-act play *The Man from Minnesota*?

A. Charlie Lutefisk.

———◆———

Q. Dvořak wrote notes for his *Opus 100, the Indian Maiden* on what item that was barely saved from obliteration?

A. His shirt cuff.

———◆———

Q. What did Red Wing native Frances Densmore preserve in photos and recordings?

A. American Indian heritage.

———◆———

Q. What recording studio's first three records, red vinyl EPs, were by local bands the Spooks, Fingerprints, and the Suburbs?

A. Twin/Tone.

Q. Where did Kris Kamm, who plays Stuart on "Coach," attend high school?

A. Wayzata.

———◆———

Q. What is the Twin Cities' oldest community theater?

A. Theatre in the Round Players.

———◆———

Q. What did Minnesota magician Dan Witkowski materialize before an audience of six thousand?

A. The Rockettes (all thirty-six of them).

———◆———

Q. Who recorded "Let It Be" in 1984?

A. The Replacements.

———◆———

Q. What happened to the Turner Hall in New Ulm the morning after Senator Hubert Humphrey spoke there in 1952?

A. It burned down.

———◆———

Q. Jon and Marcia Pankake played folk music with what group?

A. Uncle Willy and The Brandy Snifters.

———◆———

Q. Governor Rudy Perpich turned down an opportunity to sing "Hail! Minnesota!" with other governors for whose television special in 1985?

A. David Letterman.

Q. For what did University of Minnesota composer Dominick Argento receive a 1975 Pulitzer Prize?

A. *From the Diary of Virginia Woolf.*

Q. What group held a cultural exchange with the Moscow Central Children's Theatre in 1989?

A. The Children's Theatre Company.

Q. What historian, television commentator, and *New York Times* journalist is a Minneapolis native?

A. Harrison Salisbury.

Q. What director of "Nobody's Child" and "Intimate Strangers" moved to Shafer and began training as a Hazelden counselor?

A. Elly Sidel.

Q. What theatre opened with a world premiere of George Bernard Shaw's *The Dark Lady of the Sonnets* on November 17, 1914?

A. The Duluth Little Theatre (now the Duluth Playhouse).

Q. What was the Suburbs' first national hit?

A. "Music for Boys."

Q. How much was Bob Dylan paid for his first record?

A. Four hundred dollars.

Q. Who tended Clellan Card on "Axel and His Dog"?

A. Mary Davies Orfield (as Nurse Carmen).

———◆———

Q. Who helped establish both the Muppet Players and At the Foot of the Mountain (AFM), a women's theater?

A. Martha Boesing.

———◆———

Q. When did Hüsker Dü break up?

A. 1988.

———◆———

Q. What Minnesota musician was the first to combine a guitar with a harmonica in a frame-holder?

A. Bob Dylan.

———◆———

Q. Where did Sharon Anderson appear before beginning her tenure on "Good Company"?

A. The Old Log Theatre.

———◆———

Q. The Aulger Brothers Players Company, one of the last tent shows to tour, was based where?

A. Mankato.

———◆———

Q. What Golden Valley actress, who attended the University of Minnesota for one week, starred in the 1989 movie *Drugstore Cowboy*?

A. Kelly Lynch.

Q. What was the unlikely title of the Trashmen's only hit?

A. "Surfin' Bird" (1964).

———◆———

Q. Where was most of Prince's 1984 movie *Purple Rain* filmed?

A. First Avenue.

———◆———

Q. What two writer-illustrators have designated The Children's Theatre as the only authorized producer of stage adaptations of their work?

A. Tomie dePaola and Dr. Seuss (Theodore Geisel).

———◆———

Q. Who did Bobby Velline become?

A. Bobby Vee.

———◆———

Q. With George Grizzard as Hamlet and Ellen Geer as Ophelia in the Guthrie's opening production in 1963, who played Gertrude?

A. Jessica Tandy.

———◆———

Q. What are Twin/Tone and Jungleland?

A. Minnesota music production houses.

———◆———

Q. What movie set in Minnesota mistakenly placed mountains just outside the Twin Cities?

A. *The Heartbreak Kid* (1972).

Q. What group had two *Billboard* Top 40 hits, "Jungle Love" and "The Bird," in 1985?

A. The Time.

◆

Q. What is one of the top three Irish music showcases in the country?

A. St. Paul's Half-Time Rec.

◆

Q. What turned the Orpheum into an ice rink in less than 24 hours, using 3 miles of tubing and 3,740 gallons of water?

A. Flex-Ice.

◆

Q. How many gold or platinum albums and singles did Flyte Tyme Production produce in its first five years?

A. Eighteen.

◆

Q. What was Louie Anderson's birth order in a family of eleven children?

A. Number ten.

◆

Q. What CBS correspondent attended the University of Minnesota?

A. Harry Reasoner.

◆

Q. What movie about a famous horse was set in Minnesota?

A. *The Great Dan Patch* (1949).

Q. What restaurant did Mary Tyler Moore immortalize in a television show opening sequence?

A. Vista Marquette's Jolliet restaurant.

———◆———

Q. Who produced *Big Hits of Mid-America, Vol. IV*, in 1986?

A. Twin/Tone.

———◆———

Q. Where did Duddley Riggs perform in his youth?

A. The Greatest Show on Earth.

———◆———

Q. What was the Replacements' first MTV release?

A. "Don't Tell a Soul" (1989).

———◆———

Q. What WCCO radio star was the most widely known—and the highest paid—local radio correspondent in the United States for twenty-seven years?

A. Cedric Adams.

———◆———

Q. What was first Uncle Sam's and then Sam's?

A. First Avenue.

———◆———

Q. What movie starring Patty Duke did Elisabeth Congdon allow to be filmed in her mansion in 1972?

A. *You'll Like My Mother.*

Q. Where did Marlon Brando attend boarding school?

A. Shattuck Military School, Faribault.

———◆———

Q. What Minnesota reggae group won a competition for best amateur band in Japan?

A. Ipso Facto.

———◆———

Q. What was held in Grand Rapids June 10–18, 1989?

A. A celebration for the fiftieth anniversary of *The Wizard of Oz*.

———◆———

Q. What 1985 movie starring Emilio Estevez was filmed in the Twin Cities?

A. *That Was Then, This Is Now.*

———◆———

Q. What is the occupation of former Minnesotan Shirley Witherspoon?

A. Jazz singer.

———◆———

Q. What Minnesotans wrote *Raising Arizona*?

A. Joel and Ethan Coen (Joel directed and Ethan produced).

———◆———

Q. What star of "The Man from U.N.C.L.E." attended the University of Minnesota?

A. Robert Vaughn.

HISTORY

C H A P T E R   T H R E E

Q. What St. Olaf graduate was the youngest woman elected to the Minnesota state senate?

A. Ember Reichgott (age twenty-nine when she was elected in 1983).

———◆———

Q. Although it cost $750,000 to build the James J. Hill Stone Arch Bridge in 1883, how much did Burlington Northern sell it for in 1989?

A. One dollar (to the Hennepin County Regional Transit Authority).

———◆———

Q. What Minnesota congressman sponsored the Prohibition amendment?

A. Andrew Volstead of Granite Falls.

———◆———

Q. What does IDS stand for?

A. Investors Diversified Services.

———◆———

Q. How much is a cup of coffee at the Gustavus Adolphus canteen?

A. A nickel (the same price as it was in 1949).

Q. What was the first law to ban smoking except in designated areas?

A. Minnesota's Clean Indoor Air Act (1975).

———◆———

Q. What was the name of the ten-foot sailboat in which Twin Citian Gerry Spiess crossed the Atlantic in 1979?

A. *Yankee Girl.*

———◆———

Q. How many times has Concordia College in Moorhead been visited by King Olav V of Norway?

A. Three (1939, 1968, and 1982).

———◆———

Q. Where did Zebulon Pike raise the American flag for the first time in what is now Minnesota?

A. Leech Lake (1805).

———◆———

Q. Who was known as the "Teflon governor" because bad press tended to slide off his image?

A. Rudy Perpich.

———◆———

Q. What percentage of Minnesota's high school students go on to postsecondary education?

A. 66 percent.

———◆———

Q. What was the first city in the nation to ban cigarette vending machines?

A. White Bear Lake.

Q. Why were 2,173 people arrested in Minnesota between July 1, 1922 and June 30, 1923?

A. Liquor-law violations.

———◆———

Q. What ethnic group outnumbered the English, Irish, and Swedish in Minnesota for most of the nineteenth century?

A. The Germans.

———◆———

Q. How many of America's Fortune 500 companies were based in Minnesota in 1988?

A. Eighteen.

———◆———

Q. Dave Oferosky camps over the Water Veil sculpture in St. Paul from Thanksgiving through New Year's Day to help what group?

A. The homeless.

———◆———

Q. What group of striking bank workers was the subject of a television movie?

A. The Willmar Eight.

———◆———

Q. What began as the Concerned Indian Americans in Minneapolis in July of 1968?

A. AIM (American Indian Movement).

———◆———

Q. What was the nickname of Charles A. Lindbergh, who was brought up in Little Falls?

A. "The Lone Eagle."

Q. What was Elsa Seidemann the first woman in Minnesota to receive?

A. A driver's license.

———◆———

Q. In 1949, St. Olaf was the first Lutheran college to house what academic honor society?

A. Phi Beta Kappa.

———◆———

Q. Late in the nineteenth century, Minnesota was one of the major producers of what tobacco product?

A. Cigars.

———◆———

Q. In 1992, what state had a higher percentage of registered voters than Minnesota?

A. Maine (Minnesota led in 1980–1988).

———◆———

Q. In relation to other states, what was Minnesota's rank for teenage pregnancies in 1990?

A. Lowest in the nation.

———◆———

Q. Who was the first to sign the Treaty of Mendota in 1851, which completed the sale of Sioux land to the United States?

A. Chief Little Crow.

———◆———

Q. How many of the thirteen Minneapolis council members were women in 1990?

A. Eight.

Q. Who brought suit against Carleton College for being too liberal?

A. William Bell Riley.

———◆———

Q. When did the first steamboat reach Minnesota?

A. 1842.

———◆———

Q. How many cities in Minnesota do not permit alcohol sales within their borders?

A. Sixty-two.

———◆———

Q. What former attorney was convicted of arranging his wife's murder in the 1960s?

A. T. Eugene Thompson.

———◆———

Q. What mail-order retailer was born in Waterville in 1863?

A. Richard Sears.

———◆———

Q. Who was the first white man allowed access to the Pipestone quarry?

A. George Catlin.

———◆———

Q. What organization did Chippewa Indians in Minnesota turn to in seeking restoration of treaty rights?

A. The United Nations.

Q. What does BAV, started by Joan Fluelly and Chris Bandettini, stand for?

A. Born-Again Virgin.

———————◆———————

Q. Who defeated Rudy Perpich in his 1978 gubernatorial bid?

A. Al Quie.

———————◆———————

Q. Where is the world's largest manufacturer of calendars?

A. St. Paul.

———————◆———————

Q. What Northern Pacific engineer rescued fifty residents of Hinckley from the 1894 fire?

A. Jim Root.

———————◆———————

Q. In 1985, the U.S. government agreed to pay how much in an out of court settlement to Leech Lake Ojibway Indians for tribal land taken a century earlier?

A. $3,390,288.

———————◆———————

Q. What was it illegal to sell, barter, or give away in Minnesota from 1909 to 1913?

A. Cigarettes.

———————◆———————

Q. Of all the robbers in the James–Younger raid on the bank of Northfield, who were the only ones not captured or killed?

A. Jesse and Frank James.

Q. What private liberal arts college, founded in St. Peter in 1862, is one of the oldest educational institutions in the United States?

A. Gustavus Adolphus College.

Q. Who organized the 1934 truck drivers' strike in the Twin Cities?

A. The Dunne brothers.

Q. Who was the target of an assassination attempt in 1884 in St. Paul's Grand Opera House?

A. Sitting Bull.

Q. What high honor was awarded to Norman Borlaug, a University of Minnesota alumnus, in 1972?

A. The Nobel Peace Prize, for his role in the "green revolution."

Q. Among metropolitan areas of one million or more, what is the only city to rank higher than the Twin Cities in number of ten-million-dollar corporations per capita?

A. Boston.

Q. What railroad magnate built the Great Northern line?

A. James J. Hill.

Q. What was the Endotronics scandal called?

A. Endogate.

Q. Who was responsible for building the cathedral of St. Paul?

A. Bishop Ireland.

———◆———

Q. Where was the Depot Hotel, gathering place for lumberjacks that could seat five hundred in its two dining rooms?

A. Hinckley.

———◆———

Q. Who claimed credit for many of La Salle's discoveries in the book *New Discovery of a Very Great Region Situated in America,* published in 1697 after La Salle's death?

A. Father Louis Hennepin, a Belgian missionary.

———◆———

Q. What did William Bell Riley found in 1922?

A. The Minnesota Anti-Evolution League.

———◆———

Q. What former police chief was made the Minnesota gambling czar?

A. Tony Bouza.

———◆———

Q. When was the first store opened in St. Paul?

A. 1842.

———◆———

Q. What two corporations were started by Hibbing resident Jeno Palucci?

A. Chun King and Jeno's Pizza.

Q. What annual event did St. Olaf College host in 1989, which will rotate among five Midwest Evangelical Lutheran colleges?

A. The Nobel Peace Prize forum (St. Olaf's, Augsburg, Luther, Concordia [Moorhead], and Augustana in South Dakota).

◆

Q. When did St. Paul become capital of the Minnesota Territory?

A. 1849.

◆

Q. Who was the driving force behind the Mall of America in Bloomington?

A. The Ghermezian brothers.

◆

Q. What town has been home to five Minnesota governors?

A. St. Peter.

◆

Q. What does *Minnesota* mean in the Sioux Indian language?

A. "Sky-tinted waters."

◆

Q. Who is thought to have used the anchor stones on Big Cormorant Lake to secure their ships?

A. Early Norse explorers.

◆

Q. What state was the first to offer troops for the Civil War to Abraham Lincoln?

A. Minnesota.

Q. What town served as the center of Indian missions after a church and school were established in 1859?

A. Faribault.

———◆———

Q. What is the area south of a line from Eau Claire to Brainerd to Sioux Falls called?

A. The "industrial triangle."

———◆———

Q. What "perennial candidate" for the presidency ran first in 1948 and as late as 1988?

A. Harold Stassen.

———◆———

Q. What percentage of Minnesotans graduate from high school, well over the national average of 71 percent?

A. Ninety-one percent.

———◆———

Q. What was the site of the first permanent white settlement in Minnesota?

A. Mendota.

———◆———

Q. How much money per acre were the Sioux offered for twenty-four million acres of land in the Treaty of Travers de Sioux?

A. A little over twelve cents per acre to be paid over fifty years.

———◆———

Q. How many of the fifty congressmen to vote against declaring war on Germany in 1917 were from Minnesota?

A. Four.

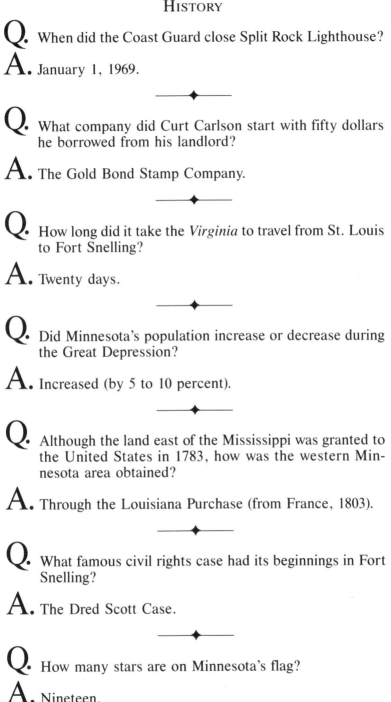

Q. When did the Coast Guard close Split Rock Lighthouse?

A. January 1, 1969.

———◆———

Q. What company did Curt Carlson start with fifty dollars he borrowed from his landlord?

A. The Gold Bond Stamp Company.

———◆———

Q. How long did it take the *Virginia* to travel from St. Louis to Fort Snelling?

A. Twenty days.

———◆———

Q. Did Minnesota's population increase or decrease during the Great Depression?

A. Increased (by 5 to 10 percent).

———◆———

Q. Although the land east of the Mississippi was granted to the United States in 1783, how was the western Minnesota area obtained?

A. Through the Louisiana Purchase (from France, 1803).

———◆———

Q. What famous civil rights case had its beginnings in Fort Snelling?

A. The Dred Scott Case.

———◆———

Q. How many stars are on Minnesota's flag?

A. Nineteen.

Q. Who was elected mayor of Minneapolis in 1945?

A. Hubert H. Humphrey.

———◆———

Q. Why did Minneapolis and St. Paul kidnap each other's census takers in the mid-to-late 1800s?

A. To try to prevent one from outgrowing the other.

———◆———

Q. Why was Minneapolis known as "Mill City" in the late 1800s?

A. It produced such huge quantities of flour.

———◆———

Q. Which airline is headquartered at the Minneapolis–St. Paul International Airport?

A. Northwest Orient.

———◆———

Q. What head of state visited Minnesota on June 3, 1990?

A. Mikhail Gorbachev.

———◆———

Q. Who treated New Ulm victims of an 1862 Indian attack?

A. Dr. W. W. Mayo.

———◆———

Q. Where did James Green build the first dam and sawmill across the Mississippi in 1849?

A. Little Falls.

Q. The Patrons of Husbandry, founded in St. Paul in 1867 by government clerk Oliver Hudson Kelley and six associates, is popularly known as what?

A. The Grange.

◆

Q. Why did Harold Stassen resign early in his third term as governor?

A. To serve in the U.S. Navy.

◆

Q. The 1964 state constitutional taconite amendment guaranteed that taconite producers would have a twenty-five-year period free from what?

A. Tax increases.

◆

Q. Who rescued Father Louis Hennepin from the Sioux in 1680?

A. Daniel Greysolon, Sieur Duluth.

◆

Q. Who ordered the victorious Civil War charge up Missionary Ridge at Chattanooga, Tennessee, in which the Second Minnesota participated?

A. No one.

◆

Q. Where did the steamer *Seawing* capsize, killing ninety-eight passengers?

A. Lake Pepin.

◆

Q. What Christian Indian sheltered white refugees in an old building and led them to safety during the 1862 Sioux uprising?

A. John Other Day.

Q. What was chartered in 1851, seven years before Minnesota became a state?

A. The University of Minnesota.

Q. What did Le Sueur think the two tons of blue-colored earth he transported to France were?

A. Copper ore (it turned out to be worthless clay).

Q. What did Archbishop John Ireland of St. Paul fight against?

A. Alcohol.

Q. Who did Thomas Jefferson send to explore the Minnesota Territory in 1805?

A. Lieutenant Zebulon Pike.

Q. What percentage of total U.S. iron ore shipments from 1941 to 1945 were from Minnesota?

A. Seventy percent.

Q. What did Richard Green become after he left the Minneapolis school system?

A. Chancellor of the New York public schools.

Q. How many drinking establishments did Winona have during Prohibition?

A. As many as 200 (five times as many as when drinking was legal).

Q. What did the Indians call Bishop Whipple?

A. "Straight Tongue."

Q. What former U.S. Supreme Court chief justice attended the University of Minnesota?

A. Warren Burger.

Q. What St. Olaf graduates were the "typical American family" who hosted Raisa Gorbachev during her 1990 visit?

A. Steve and Karen Watson.

Q. What fort was established near the junction of the Minnesota and Mississippi rivers?

A. Fort Snelling.

Q. Who was the engineer for "Old No. 201," on display in Owatonna?

A. Casey Jones.

Q. What associate justice of the U.S. Supreme Court, born in Maine, Minnesota, in 1898, served on the court longer than any other justice?

A. William Orville Douglas.

Q. When was Ramsey Mill, the state's first flour mill, established near Hastings?

A. 1857.

Q. Who owned the Northfield Bank, which was attacked by the former Confederate guerrillas of the James-Younger band?

A. Former Union Generals Butler and Ames.

———◆———

Q. What was thought to be one of the main causes of the Sioux uprising of 1862?

A. The Treaty of Travers de Sioux.

———◆———

Q. What Minnesota political figure was on *People* magazine's list of the Twenty-five Most Intriguing People of 1984?

A. Kathleen Morris (Scott County attorney).

———◆———

Q. Who was known as the Squire of Mendota?

A. Henry Hastings Sibley.

———◆———

Q. What University of Minnesota professor of rhetoric and elocution from 1880 to 1909 was the first American woman to be named a full professor?

A. Maria L. Sanford.

———◆———

Q. Where did former governor Al Quie attend college?

A. St. Olaf.

———◆———

Q. How many Minnesota regiments fought in the Civil War battle of Nashville?

A. Four.

Q. What was John Other Day awarded by Congress for saving white refugees from the Sioux?

A. $2,500.

———◆———

Q. What year was the Minnesota state capitol in St. Paul dedicated?

A. 1905.

———◆———

Q. Who was the embattled University of Minnesota president before Nils Hasselmo?

A. Ken Keller.

———◆———

Q. After consisting of less than five thousand people in 1849, what had the Minnesota population grown to by 1860?

A. 172,000.

———◆———

Q. What did Indian agent Major Lawrence Taliaferro forbid in trying to keep the fur trade under control?

A. Liquor.

———◆———

Q. What town almost became the state capital when it was thought Minnesota would be an east-west facing state?

A. St. Peter.

———◆———

Q. What is the state motto?

A. L'Étoile du Nord (French for "Star of the North").

Q. Fur trader William Morrison claimed to be the first to discover what in 1804, years before Henry Schoolcraft?

A. The headwaters of the Mississippi.

Q. Who was secretary of state under Calvin Coolidge, 1925–29?

A. Rochester resident Frank Billings Kellogg.

Q. Where did Walter Mondale attend college?

A. The University of Minnesota.

Q. What were Jim Root's hands seared to during the 1894 Hinckley fire?

A. The throttle of his train.

Q. What did Henry H. Sibley build—a first west of the Mississippi—known as the "Mount Vernon of Minnesota"?

A. The first stone house.

Q. What steamboat traveled 265 miles in 24 hours and 40 minutes, averaging 13 miles per hour while underway?

A. The *Grey Eagle*.

Q. What Carleton graduate was the first woman ambassador from the United States?

A. Eugenie Anderson.

Q. When did Minnesota become a state?

A. May 11, 1858.

———◆———

Q. What St. Paul surveyor claimed to be the first Union volunteer in the Civil War?

A. Josias R. King (Pioneer Guards).

———◆———

Q. What did Karl Rölvaag, son of author Ole Rölvaag, become?

A. Governor of Minnesota.

———◆———

Q. Who established the first mill in Minnesota in 1845, using part of his wife's dress in the sifting process?

A. Lemuel Boles.

———◆———

Q. Who was known as the "elder statesman of liberalism"?

A. Hubert H. Humphrey.

———◆———

Q. When Minnesota became a state, how many states were already in the union?

A. Thirty-one.

———◆———

Q. Where did Joseph Rolette hide the bill, until the constitutional time limit had passed, that would have changed the state capital to St. Peter?

A. In a hotel room.

Q. How many people immigrated to Minnesota from other states in July 1855?

A. Over one thousand.

Q. What was the William Crooks?

A. Minnesota's first locomotive.

Q. Although the Kellogg-Briand Pact was an unsuccessful attempt to curb war, what did Minnesota's Frank Billings Kellogg win in 1929?

A. The Nobel Peace Prize.

Q. What city had a three-day gold rush in the 1860s?

A. Rochester.

Q. How many docks are there at the Duluth–Superior Harbor?

A. Ninety-nine.

Q. What town included abolition of slavery, equal rights for women, no gambling, and the establishment of the Humanities Church in its constitution?

A. Hutchinson.

Q. What private college established in 1873 is situated midway between Minneapolis and St. Paul?

A. Macalester College.

Q. Who named St. Paul?

A. Father Galtier.

———◆———

Q. What U.S. representative from Colorado and 1988 presidential candidate attended the University of Minnesota?

A. Patricia Schroeder.

———◆———

Q. What was the original name of the settlement that became St. Paul?

A. Pig's Eye (for the French-Canadian whiskey trader, Pierre "Pig's Eye" Parrant, who had led squatters to the spot).

———◆———

Q. What uncle and partner of Charles Pillsbury was state senator from 1864 to 1876 and governor of Minnesota from 1876 to 1882?

A. John Sargent.

———◆———

Q. What did Jane Swisshelm, the editor of the newspaper at St. Cloud, crusade against?

A. Slavery.

———◆———

Q. What city sought an injunction against Duluth's attempt to dig a channel through Minnesota Point, causing Duluth to dig furiously before it could be served?

A. Superior, Wisconsin.

———◆———

Q. Henry M. Rice and Gen. James Shields were the first to hold what positions for Minnesota?

A. United States senators.

Q. The admission of what state slowed up Minnesota's bid for statehood?

A. Kansas.

Q. On the second day of what battle did the First Minnesota Regiment make history?

A. Gettysburg.

Q. The land comprising present-day Minnesota belonged to what two powerful Indian tribes in the 1700s and 1800s?

A. The Ojibway (Chippewa) and the Dakotah (Sioux).

Q. Until 1988, Minnesota voted for the winning side in all but how many presidential elections?

A. Four.

Q. What judge ruled on the Reserve Mining and Dalkon Shield cases?

A. Judge Miles Lord.

Q. What could be heard for miles because their wooden axles weren't greased?

A. The Red River ox carts.

Q. Who reluctantly led most of the Sioux forces against the whites in 1862?

A. Little Crow.

Q. What town was the earliest European settlement in Minnesota?

A. Grand Portage.

———◆———

Q. What secretary of the National Republican League and speaker of the Minnesota House of Representatives lost both legs, one hand, and part of the other hand in a blizzard when he was a boy?

A. Michael John Dowling.

———◆———

Q. What 1870 event caused Duluth's population to leap?

A. Completion of the railroad between St. Paul and Duluth.

———◆———

Q. When was the Pipestone National Monument established?

A. 1937.

———◆———

Q. What community was mostly shut down in the 1857 national monetary panic?

A. Duluth.

———◆———

Q. Starting in 1844 with six, how many Red River ox carts made the journey in 1858?

A. As many as six hundred.

———◆———

Q. What is the oldest church in continuous use in Minnesota?

A. St. Peter's Catholic Church in Mendota (since 1853).

Q. What was James J. Hill known as?

A. "The Empire Builder."

---◆---

Q. In 1849 who began publishing the state's first newspaper, the *Minnesota Pioneer,* in St. Paul?

A. James Madison Goodhue.

---◆---

Q. Besides Minnesota, whose electoral votes went to Walter Mondale in the 1984 presidential election?

A. The District of Columbia.

---◆---

Q. Where was New Ulm's thirty-seven-bell carillon clock cast?

A. The Netherlands.

---◆---

Q. What was the claim to fame of Albert Woolson, who died August 2, 1965, in Duluth at the age of 109?

A. Last survivor of the Union army.

---◆---

Q. Who was born in Ceylon, Minnesota, on January 1, 1928?

A. Walter E. Mondale.

---◆---

Q. What eighty-three-year-old millionaire was murdered by her son-in-law with a pink satin pillow on June 17, 1977?

A. Elisabeth Congdon (her nurse was murdered also).

Q. How long did it take the Red River ox carts to travel between the Red River settlements and St. Paul?

A. Thirty to forty days.

———◆———

Q. Who was the first teacher in St. Paul's first school of historic importance?

A. Miss Harriet Bishop.

———◆———

Q. After debts to traders absorbed all but $880 of the Sioux's first payment, how much of the last $96,000 owed to the Indians after the Travers de Sioux was actually paid?

A. None.

———◆———

Q. What had more losses than any other Northern regiment in the First Battle of Bull Run in the Civil War?

A. The First Minnesota Regiment.

———◆———

Q. Why wasn't Joseph Lee Heywood able to unlock the safe at the First National Bank in Northfield before he was murdered in the James-Younger robbery?

A. It was already unlocked.

———◆———

Q. How many public schools were there in Minnesota in 1849?

A. Three.

———◆———

Q. Where was John Jacob Astor's greatest fur trading post?

A. Mendota.

Q. In 1870, Jay Cooke decided to support the construction of a Northern Pacific line connecting Duluth with what?

A. The Pacific Ocean.

———◆———

Q. Where was Minnesota's first teacher training institute, or normal school, established in 1860?

A. Winona.

———◆———

Q. By the close of 1869, Minnesota had how many of the forty-nine local granges in the United States?

A. Forty.

———◆———

Q. Where was St. Paul's Hamline University originally located?

A. Red Wing.

———◆———

Q. What did prohibitionist Andrew Volstead consume in quantities of nearly a pound a day at times?

A. Chewing tobacco.

———◆———

Q. Eighteen men were killed in an 1878 explosion of what type of businesses?

A. Minneapolis flour mills.

———◆———

Q. What was established in 1849, nine years before Minnesota became a state?

A. The state historical society.

Q. What was the only Minnesota army post to remain in active service through the Spanish–American War and both world wars?

A. Fort Snelling.

---◆---

Q. What daring Minnesotan was the first to fly solo nonstop across the Atlantic?

A. Charles A. Lindbergh, Jr. (New York to Paris, 1927).

---◆---

Q. One of the finest inland harbors in the world, the Duluth–Superior harbor encompasses how many square miles?

A. Nineteen.

---◆---

Q. What did Minnesotan George Moran become in the twenties?

A. A gangster.

---◆---

Q. What party helped elect Floyd B. Olson as governor in the 1930's?

A. The Farmer-Labor party.

---◆---

Q. The University of Minnesota was one of the first in the nation to include what pharmaceutical products in snack vending machines?

A. Condoms.

---◆---

Q. Whose son was the victim of a famous kidnapping and murder in 1932?

A. Charles A. Lindbergh, Jr., and Anne Morrow Lindbergh's.

Q. What is William Williams' claim to fame?

A. He was the last person hanged in Minnesota, February 13, 1906.

———◆———

Q. How many state capitol buildings did Minnesota have before the current one?

A. Two.

———◆———

Q. Where did one of the nation's greatest forest fires occur on September 1, 1894?

A. Hinckley.

———◆———

Q. Who is the wealthiest man in Minnesota, with 925 million dollars in early 1990?

A. Curt Carlson.

———◆———

Q. How many Minnesotans lost their lives in World War II?

A. Six thousand.

———◆———

Q. What year did the St. Lawrence Seaway open, allowing ocean-going ships to come to Duluth?

A. 1959.

———◆———

Q. What did trader Myrick say to starving Indians who had come to ask for food or credit?

A. "Let them eat grass."

Q. What does G.T.A. stand for?

A. Grain Terminal Association.

———◆———

Q. What special stone was found on the farm of Olaf Ohman, near Alexandria, in 1898?

A. The Kensington runestone, whose carvings allegedly tell of a journey of a band of Vikings in 1362.

———◆———

Q. What family lost their mineral rights to the giant steel corporations in the financial panic of 1893?

A. The Merritts.

———◆———

Q. How many people died in the 1894 Hinckley fire?

A. Over four hundred.

———◆———

Q. Who said, "What you farmers need is to raise less corn and more hell"?

A. Mary Lease.

———◆———

Q. How many of the 262 members of the First Minnesota Regiment escaped injury or death in a suicidal charge at Gettysburg?

A. Forty-seven.

———◆———

Q. With male teachers making $16.25 a month in 1862, how much did female teachers make?

A. Twelve dollars a month.

Q. Until 1971, what town's historical society retained the skull of Chief Little Crow, who died after he was shot five miles west of town while picking berries with his son?

A. Hutchinson.

＊

Q. What was trader Myrick's mouth stuffed with after he was killed by the Sioux?

A. Grass.

＊

Q. How many of Fort Snelling's original fifteen buildings still exist?

A. Four (the round tower, the hexagonal tower, the commandant's house, and the officers' quarters).

＊

Q. What kind of rumor started Ely, the popular resort?

A. The discovery of gold (which turned out to be iron).

＊

Q. What did the mansion of Swan J. Turnblad become?

A. The American Swedish Institute.

＊

Q. How long was Lindbergh's May 1927 flight, for which he was awarded $25,000?

A. Thirty hours.

＊

Q. What landmark majority opinion of the U.S. Supreme Court did Harry Blackmun, who grew up in St. Paul, write?

A. *Roe v. Wade* (1973).

ARTS & LITERATURE

C H A P T E R   F O U R

Q. Who collaborated on *Killing Time in St. Cloud,* published in 1988?

A. Minnesotans Judith Guest and Rebecca Hill.

———◆———

Q. Where does well-known science fiction and fantasy artist Erin McKee live?

A. Minneapolis.

———◆———

Q. Who published Rochester writer Harriet Hodgson's *A Parent's Survival Guide: How to Cope When Your Kid Is Using Drugs?*

A. Hazelden and Harper & Row.

———◆———

Q. What ten-pound, six-ounce baby was born in St. Paul in September of 1896?

A. Francis Scott Key Fitzgerald.

———◆———

Q. What cartoonist was born on November 26, 1922, in Minneapolis?

A. Charles Schulz.

Q. What did Eleanor Arnason's Minneapolis housewife character turn into in a 1987 novel?

A. A bear *(Daughter of the Bear King)*.

———◆———

Q. What is Minnesotan Mary Ellen Pinkham famous for?

A. Household hints.

———◆———

Q. Whose first book was *If I Die in a Combat Zone, Box Me Up and Ship Me Home?*

A. Tim O'Brien.

———◆———

Q. What artistic walkway by Siah Armajani crosses sixteen lanes of traffic between Loring Park and the Minneapolis Sculpture Garden?

A. The Irene Hixon Whitney Bridge.

———◆———

Q. For what line of books did Twin Cities' fantasy writers Kara Dalkey, Steven Brust, and Patricia Wrede all write novels?

A. Fairy Tales (for Ace and Tor books).

———◆———

Q. What Minnesota writer was as colorful as his character Gatsby?

A. F. Scott Fitzgerald.

———◆———

Q. What leading literary agency is based in Minneapolis?

A. The Lazear Agency.

Q. What type of books does Minnesotan LaVyrle Spencer write?

A. Bestselling romances.

———◆———

Q. Where did author Bill Holm serve as a Fullbright lecturer in American literature?

A. The University of Iceland in Reykjavik.

———◆———

Q. What is Minnesota-born sculptor James Earle Fraser's best known work, created when he was twenty years old?

A. *The End of the Trail* (1896).

———◆———

Q. Where did *Beet Queen* author Louise Erdrich and her family spend most of 1985?

A. Northfield.

———◆———

Q. What Minnesota writer has been named to the Isaak Walton Hall of Fame (1963) and awarded the Sierra Club's John Muir Award (1967)?

A. Sigurd Olson.

———◆———

Q. What type of humor did John Louis Anderson portray as mythical in a book title?

A. *Scandinavian Humor and Other Myths*.

———◆———

Q. What Minnesota author of *After We Lost Our Way* won the 1988 Poetry Series contest?

A. David Mura.

Q. Who was the director of the world-famous Walker Art Center for twenty-eight years?

A. Martin Friedman.

———◆———

Q. Who wrote *Feed Me! I'm Yours* and *The Taming of the Candy Monster?*

A. Minnesotan Vicky Lansky.

———◆———

Q. Where is the largest collection of dime novels and other similar works for boys and girls?

A. The Hess Collection (University of Minnesota).

———◆———

Q. Who wrote the best-selling historical romances *Shanna* and *A Rose in Winter?*

A. Minnesotan Kathleen Woodiwiss.

———◆———

Q. For what was Tim O'Brien awarded the National Book Award?

A. *Going after Cacciato* (1980).

———◆———

Q. Where did science fiction writer Poul Anderson attend college?

A. The University of Minnesota.

———◆———

Q. What Minnesota-published magazine is the fastest growing general interest magazine?

A. *The Utne Reader.*

Q. What was Jon Hassler's 1987 novel, based on a fictionalized Plainview?

A. *Grand Opening.*

—————◆—————

Q. What Minnesota authors wrote the thriller *The House That Fear Built* under the name Cassandra Knye?

A. Thomas M. Disch and John Sladek.

—————◆—————

Q. What is the only undergraduate liberal arts college in the United States accredited in all four fine arts (art, dance, music, and theater)?

A. St. Olaf College.

—————◆—————

Q. What did poet and author Patricia Hampl found in 1973?

A. *Minnesota Monthly* (then called *Previews*).

—————◆—————

Q. Where was Anton Gág's painting of the Sioux massacre at New Ulm placed?

A. The Minnesota State Capitol rotunda.

—————◆—————

Q. What journalist, born in Minneapolis and a graduate of the University of Minnesota, was awarded a Pulitzer Prize for *Russia Reviewed*?

A. Harrison Salisbury (1955).

—————◆—————

Q. Who wrote the critically acclaimed play *Scheherezade*?

A. Marisha Chamberlain.

Q. How many Minnesotans placed in the top 25 out of 1,370 entries in the 1980–81 federal duck stamp contest?

A. Eight.

Q. What Macalester professor was responsible for Artball Cards and Holy Holy Art Cards?

A. Don Celender.

Q. What did Harrison Salisbury originate?

A. The *New York Times* Op-Ed page.

Q. Who wrote *Wheat That Springeth Green,* nominated for the National Book Award in 1988?

A. J. F. Powers.

Q. What award-winning advertising agency is based in the Twin Cities?

A. Fallon McElligot Rice.

Q. In what subject does Bill Jack, waiter, attorney, and author of *To the Devil,* have a Ph.D.?

A. Russian literature.

Q. What Minnesota author, born in Biwabik, won O. Henry short story awards in 1961 and 1963?

A. Shirley Schoonover.

Q. Where is the only Frank Lloyd Wright-designed gas station?

A. Cloquet.

———◆———

Q. How tall is Minneapolis fantasy author Kara Dalkey?

A. Four feet, ten and three-fourths inches.

———◆———

Q. Who wrote the Newbery Honor Book *Dogsong*?

A. Gary Paulsen (1985).

———◆———

Q. In what language did St. Olaf College graduate and faculty member Ole Rölvaag first write all his works?

A. Norwegian.

———◆———

Q. Who wrote *Letters to the Country*, published in 1981?

A. Carol Bly.

———◆———

Q. What 1920 Nobel Prize winner spent considerable time in Minnesota in the early 1880s?

A. Knut Hamsun.

———◆———

Q. What famous Minnesotan is an advocate for Shy Person's Rights?

A. Garrison Keillor.

Q. In what year was the St. Paul Winter Carnival palace the largest ice structure ever built?

A. 1888 (55,000 ice blocks).

◆

Q. Where did poet Deborah Keenan, author of *The Only Window That Counts*, graduate from college?

A. Macalester.

◆

Q. Who wrote *Laughing Your Way to Good Health*?

A. Comic Susan Vass.

◆

Q. What author of *American Beauty* lived in the Twin Cities for five years?

A. C. J. Hribal.

◆

Q. What 1937 Laura Ingalls Wilder book is set in Minnesota in 1873?

A. *On the Banks of Plum Creek* (Walnut Grove).

◆

Q. Where is the largest urban sculpture garden in the world?

A. The Walker Art Center (the Minneapolis Sculpture Garden).

◆

Q. Who was one of Minnesota's earliest writers, whose description of Minnehaha Falls was used by Longfellow in the poem *The Song of Hiawatha*?

A. Mary Eastman.

Q. Where was Adolph Dehn, one of the nation's foremost watercolor artists, born?

A. Waterville.

◆

Q. Who wrote *Divine Invasions,* a biography of Philip K. Dick?

A. Minneapolis resident Lawrence Sutin.

◆

Q. Who attended the University of Minnesota and wrote for the *Star-Tribune* in 1936–37, before becoming a famous news correspondent?

A. Eric Sevareid.

◆

Q. What Twin Cities fantasy author of *Talking to Dragons* is a vegetarian?

A. Patricia Wrede.

◆

Q. Where was author and illustrator Wanda Gág born in 1893?

A. New Ulm.

◆

Q. Luther Northwestern Theological Seminary has the largest Midwest exhibit of what type of sculpture?

A. Shona stone sculpture from Africa.

◆

Q. How many ways did parenting expert Vicky Lansky come up with for telling children you love them?

A. 101 (*101 Ways to Tell Your Child "I Love You"*).

Q. What Minneapolis resident is the author of the *Guardian of the Flame* series?

A. Joel Rosenberg.

———◆———

Q. What author spent time in Hollywood as an actress and stuntwoman on such shows as *The Perils of Pauline* and *Last of the Mohicans*?

A. Meridel LeSueur (1920–28).

———◆———

Q. What area is the basis for Walter O'Meara's *We Made It through the Winter,* published in 1974?

A. Cloquet.

———◆———

Q. What 1983 Gary Paulsen novel, an ALA Best Book for Young Adults, is set in Minnesota?

A. *Dancing Carl.*

———◆———

Q. Who was the owner of one of the finest collections of modern French paintings in the world?

A. James J. Hill.

———◆———

Q. What author of *The Cape Ann* moved to Lake Calhoun?

A. Faith Sullivan.

———◆———

Q. What did metro-area resident Greg Howard create after he quit law practice in 1978?

A. The cartoon strip "Sally Forth."

Q. Who was the first American to win the Nobel Prize for literature?

A. Sinclair Lewis (1930).

———✦———

Q. One of four existing ancient copies of what Polykleitos statue is at the Minneapolis Institute of Arts?

A. *The Doryphoros.*

———✦———

Q. What science fiction writer was well-known for eccentric robots, a computer pope, and *City,* a tale narrated by dogs after humans have disappeared from the Earth?

A. Clifford Simak.

———✦———

Q. Who wrote *How to Talk Minnesotan?*

A. Howard Mohr.

———✦———

Q. What statue is said to be the nation's most photographed?

A. Paul Bunyan and Babe (in Brainerd).

———✦———

Q. What Adrian native published *Poor Cedric's Almanac* in 1952?

A. Cedric Adams.

———✦———

Q. Where is the fountain "Spoonbridge and Cherry"?

A. The Minneapolis Sculpture Garden.

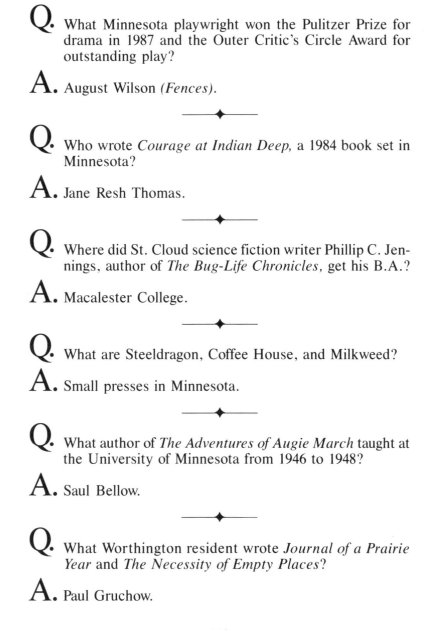

Q. Who illustrated Mary Eastman's books?

A. Her husband, Seth Eastman.

———✦———

Q. What Minnesota playwright won the Pulitzer Prize for drama in 1987 and the Outer Critic's Circle Award for outstanding play?

A. August Wilson *(Fences)*.

———✦———

Q. Who wrote *Courage at Indian Deep,* a 1984 book set in Minnesota?

A. Jane Resh Thomas.

———✦———

Q. Where did St. Cloud science fiction writer Phillip C. Jennings, author of *The Bug-Life Chronicles,* get his B.A.?

A. Macalester College.

———✦———

Q. What are Steeldragon, Coffee House, and Milkweed?

A. Small presses in Minnesota.

———✦———

Q. What author of *The Adventures of Augie March* taught at the University of Minnesota from 1946 to 1948?

A. Saul Bellow.

———✦———

Q. What Worthington resident wrote *Journal of a Prairie Year* and *The Necessity of Empty Places?*

A. Paul Gruchow.

Q. What does Dr. Albert Kuhfeld design for the mysteries his wife writes under the name Mary Monica Pulver?

A. Death traps.

———◆———

Q. What Minnesotan was the third writer to receive the Science Fiction Writers of America's Grand Master Award?

A. Clifford Simak (1977).

———◆———

Q. What 1974 work by Les Kouba started the wildlife art boom in America?

A. "Headin' for Shelter."

———◆———

Q. What poet's first published short story was included in *The Best American Short Stories 1977*?

A. Patricia Hampl ("Look at a Teacup").

———◆———

Q. The Hench collection at the Wilson Library is the largest institutional collection of what in the world?

A. Sherlock Holmes literature.

———◆———

Q. Stephen A. Douglas Volk was the first director of what institution?

A. The Minneapolis School of Art.

———◆———

Q. What book, first published in 1778, has been through fifty-three known editions in nine countries?

A. *Travels Through the Interior Parts of North-America,* by Johnathon Carver.

Q. In 1972, what poet committed suicide by jumping off a bridge in Minneapolis?

A. John Berryman.

———◆———

Q. What Twin Cities fantasy author wrote *The Blind Knight*?

A. Gail Van Asten.

———◆———

Q. What 1969 Margaret Culkin Banning book was set in northern Minnesota?

A. *Mesabi.*

———◆———

Q. Who attended Central High School and the University of Minnesota before writing *The Many Loves of Dobie Gillis*?

A. Max Shulman.

———◆———

Q. What was Judith Guest's second novel?

A. *Second Heaven.*

———◆———

Q. The sculpture *Doryphorus*, dated approximately 440 B.C., is valued at how much?

A. 2.5 million dollars.

———◆———

Q. What health columnist for the *New York Times* was a reporter for the *Minneapolis Tribune*?

A. Jane Brody.

Q. Who designed Owatonna's Northwestern National Bank in 1908?

A. Architect Louis Sullivan.

———◆———

Q. What Minnesota author of the Vietnam novel *Another War, Another Peace* is also a pediatric nephrologist?

A. Ronald J. Glasser.

———◆———

Q. Who received the Nobel Prize for literature in 1976?

A. Saul Bellow.

———◆———

Q. Where did humorist Howard Mohr teach in the English department from 1970 to 1989?

A. Southwest State University in Marshall.

———◆———

Q. What Newbery Award-winning author of *Caddie Woodlawn* lived in St. Paul?

A. Carol Ryrie Brink.

———◆———

Q. Where was sculptor Paul Manship born in 1885?

A. St. Paul.

———◆———

Q. In what Clifford Simak novel did a fifty-foot high black box from outer space land in Minnesota?

A. *The Visitors.*

Q. What was F. Scott Fitzgerald's last (unfinished) novel?

A. *The Last Tycoon.*

———◆———

Q. What Minneapolis author wrote *The Dragon in Waiting*?

A. John M. Ford.

———◆———

Q. F. Melius Christiansen, knighted by the King of Norway, was the director of music at what Minnesota college?

A. St. Olaf College.

———◆———

Q. For what work did John Berryman win the 1965 Pulitzer Prize for poetry?

A. *77 Dream Songs.*

———◆———

Q. What author from the north woods wrote *The Gift of the Deer*?

A. Helen Hoover.

———◆———

Q. Who was the first American artist to use watercolors and one of the first to use photography as an aid in his painting?

A. Seth Eastman.

———◆———

Q. What St. Paul physician wrote the 1985 novel *Pictures from a Trip*?

A. Tim Rumsey.

Q. What did Marylee Hardenbergh put on top of the Opus skyscraper in Minneapolis and on the mooring cells of the St. Anthony Falls Lock and Dam?

A. Dancers.

◆

Q. What Minnesota playwright had *Minnesota Moon* published in *Best Short Plays of 1982*?

A. John Olive.

◆

Q. Who is the narrator of Emma L. Brock's *Drusilla*?

A. A corn husk doll.

◆

Q. Where do some of Pamela Dean's fantasy novels take place?

A. The Secret Country.

◆

Q. Who wrote the occult murder mystery *Shattered Moon*?

A. Kate Green.

◆

Q. What Minnesota writer wrote *Mister Roberts*?

A. Tom Heggan.

◆

Q. Although *The Glendower Legacy* takes place in New England, what novelist set *The Wind Chill Factor* and *The Cavanaugh Quest* in Minnesota?

A. Thomas Gifford.

Q. Who coined the term "Jazz Age"?

A. F. Scott Fitzgerald.

◆

Q. Who wrote *Falling up the Stairs*?

A. James Lileks (1988).

◆

Q. What Minnesota science fiction writer taught himself to read at four and graduated from Central High in Minneapolis when he was fifteen?

A. Gordon R. Dickson.

◆

Q. Although Kouba's "Headin' for Shelter" originally sold for forty dollars, how much do prints cost now?

A. 2,500 dollars.

◆

Q. What J. F. Powers book won the National Book Award in 1963?

A. *Morte d'Urban*.

◆

Q. What Minnesota sculptor created the Buffalo nickel?

A. James Earle Fraser.

◆

Q. What Thomas M. Disch novel is set in the Twin Cities and includes the ghost of John Berryman as one of its characters?

A. *The Businessman: A Tale of Terror*.

Q. In what mythical Minnesota town would one be if "all the women are strong, the men good-looking, and the children above average"?

A. Lake Wobegon.

———✦———

Q. What winner of the Writer's of the Future Contest edits the Minnesota science fiction magazine *Tales of the Unanticipated*?

A. Eric M. Heideman.

———✦———

Q. What did Robert Bly found in 1966?

A. American Writers Against the Vietnam War.

———✦———

Q. What Nancy Carlson children's book featured a terrified dog in a tutu?

A. *Harriet's Recital.*

———✦———

Q. Where did novelist and physician Dr. Tim Rumsey attend college?

A. College of St. Thomas, St. Paul.

———✦———

Q. Why was poet Michael Denis Browne declared ineligible for a five-hundred-dollar prize for his poem "The Dream of a Soldier" in 1967?

A. He was still a British citizen at the time.

———✦———

Q. For what is Charles Gagnon famous?

A. Sculpture.

Q. What did Minneapolis native Brenda Ueland publish in 1938?

A. *If You Want to Write.*

———◆———

Q. What Minnesota poet told the story of her ancestor, John Cabell Breckenridge, who was vice president under Buchanan and Confederate secretary of war?

A. Jill Breckenridge *(Civil Blood).*

———◆———

Q. What author who was a professor at the University of Minnesota from 1942 to 1950 won the Pulitzer Prize for literature in 1947?

A. Robert Penn Warren (for *All the King's Men).*

———◆———

Q. What Minnesotan refused the Pulitzer Prize for literature in 1926?

A. Sinclair Lewis (for *Arrowsmith).*

———◆———

Q. What body of work encompasses Gordon R. Dickson's Hugo-winning novel *Soldier, Ask Not?*

A. The Childe Cycle.

———◆———

Q. What instrument does Evelina Chao, author of *Gates of Grace,* play in the St. Paul Chamber Orchestra?

A. The viola.

———◆———

Q. Where is Paul Manship's sculpture of Prometheus?

A. The sunken plaza at Rockefeller Center.

Q. For what artist was the stone at Pipestone National Monument named because he painted pictures of it and the peace pipes made from it?

A. George Catlin (catlinite).

Q. What was the former name of the *City Pages*?

A. *Sweet Potato.*

Q. What Little Falls resident and U.S. congressman wrote *Banking and Currency* and *Why Is Your Country at War?*

A. Charles Lindbergh, father of the famous flyer.

Q. What is the ethnic background of Minneapolis resident Steven Brust, author of *Cowboy Feng's Space Bar and Grille?*

A. Hungarian.

Q. What Minnesotan wrote *How to Prepare for Your High School Reunion and Other Midlife Musings?*

A. Susan Allen Toth.

Q. Who wrote the psychological crime novel *Nightmare?*

A. Marjorie Dorner.

Q. What Southwest State University faculty member co-edited the 1986 anthology *Strong Measures: Contemporary American Poetry in Traditional Forms?*

A. Philip Dacey.

Q. Twin Citian Steven Gammel won what award in 1989 for illustrating *Song and Dance Man?*

A. The Caldecott Award.

———◆———

Q. For what work was Robert Bly awarded the National Book Award in 1968?

A. *The Light around the Body.*

———◆———

Q. Zumbrota-born C. C. Beck was the creator and artist of what comic book superhero?

A. Captain Marvel.

———◆———

Q. What is Katherine Nash's "Mother and Child" made of?

A. Steel shapes welded together.

———◆———

Q. What Minnesota author wrote the medical thriller *Mindscream?*

A. R. D. Zimmerman.

———◆———

Q. The Kerlan collection contains what type of books, manuscripts, and illustrations?

A. Children's.

———◆———

Q. Where did Ole Rölvaag teach?

A. St. Olaf College in Northfield.

Q. What St. Paul science fiction writer coined the term *cyberpunk*?

A. Bruce Bethke.

———◆———

Q. What did poet Robert Bly major in at St. Olaf College before he switched to English and transferred to Harvard?

A. Pre-med.

———◆———

Q. How old was Eric Ziegenhegen when his play *Seniority* was produced after winning an award at the Young Playwrights Festival in New York?

A. Eighteen (He was sixteen when he wrote it).

———◆———

Q. With what costume-clad group is St. Louis Park resident Mary Kuhfeld, who writes mysteries as Mary Monica Pulver, involved?

A. The Society for Creative Anachronism.

———◆———

Q. Where is New York artist Leroy Neiman from?

A. St. Paul.

———◆———

Q. What style did Cameron Booth use to create *Fragrance* in 1960?

A. Abstract Expressionism.

———◆———

Q. Who wrote *Giants in the Earth*?

A. Ole Rölvaag.

Q. What book was written by an inmate of the Minnesota State Prison in Stillwater and published in 1903, two years after he was released?

A. *The Story of Cole Younger, by Himself.*

◆

Q. What percentage of Jon Hassler's fiction does he consider autobiographical?

A. Thirty-seven percent.

◆

Q. Where did artist John Flannagan spend his boyhood?

A. St. Paul.

◆

Q. Where does Susan Allen Toth teach?

A. Macalester College.

◆

Q. What Minnesota landmark was designed by Cass Gilbert, architect of the U.S. Supreme Court Building and the George Washington Bridge?

A. The state capitol.

◆

Q. What award did Minnesotan James Arlington Wright win with his *Collected Poems* in 1972?

A. The Pulitzer Prize for poetry.

◆

Q. How many birds does wildlife artist Les Kouba always place in his paintings?

A. Thirteen.

Q. Who started the Minneapolis Symphony Orchestra?

A. Emil Oberhoffer.

———◆———

Q. What Minneapolis science fiction and fantasy author wrote *The Tangled Lands* and *Cats Have No Lord*?

A. Will Shetterley.

———◆———

Q. What Apple Valley resident wrote the adventure/spy novel *The Hawthorne Conspiracy*?

A. Stephen Hesla.

———◆———

Q. After studying with Cameron Booth at the University of Minnesota, who was famous for giant works, including "Painting for the American Negro"?

A. James Rosenquist.

———◆———

Q. What was Sinclair Lewis's first name?

A. Harry.

———◆———

Q. What St. Paul building has the largest unsupported marble dome in the world?

A. The state capitol.

———◆———

Q. Poet Cary Waterman, author of *The Salamander Migration,* enrolled at what college after her children were in school?

A. Mankato State.

Q. Sir (William) Tyrone Guthrie, creator of the Guthrie Theater in Minneapolis, was one of the first to write plays for what medium?

A. Radio.

◆

Q. Who wrote *Pay Yourself What You're Worth?*

A. Shirley Hutton.

◆

Q. What street does Paul Kramer's "Apartment Walls" depict?

A. West Seventh Street in St. Paul in 1959.

◆

Q. Who has been called "the Isaac Bashevis Singer of the Chippewas"?

A. Gerald Vizenor.

◆

Q. Where is "The Four Seasons with a Sundial," a twenty-foot circle of stones with four granite boulders created by Kinji Akagaw in 1986?

A. Tettagouche State Park on the North Shore of Lake Superior.

◆

Q. What book do some people think the text of the Kensington rune stone was taken from?

A. *The Well-Informed Schoolmaster* by Carl Rosland.

◆

Q. Who created much of the state capitol's sculpture?

A. Daniel Chester French.

Q. What feminist writer was blacklisted in the McCarthy era for being involved with the radical movement?

A. Meridel LeSueur.

———◆———

Q. Where is wildlife artist Terry Redlin from?

A. Hastings.

———◆———

Q. In what fantasy novel did Emma Bull describe a fairy war in present-day Minneapolis?

A. *War for the Oaks.*

———◆———

Q. What did Mankato resident Maud Hart Lovelace write?

A. The Betsey-Tacey books.

———◆———

Q. What Minnesota author has created custom crossword puzzles?

A. Carol Bly.

———◆———

Q. Whose 1953 Pulitzer Prize-winning autobiography was titled *The Spirit of St. Louis*?

A. Charles A. Lindbergh.

———◆———

Q. What was F. Scott Fitzgerald's first book?

A. *This Side of Paradise* (1920).

Q. Who is one of the best-known fictional women in American history, created by General Mills in the 1920s?

A. Betty Crocker.

Q. Where was the birthplace of Wanda Gág, author of the children's classic, *Millions of Cats*?

A. New Ulm.

Q. Who wrote *Green Earth,* set in Minnesota and published in 1977?

A. Frederick Manfred.

Q. What choir first performed *a cappella* choral singing in the United States?

A. The St. Olaf College choir.

Q. What Minnesota poet published volume one of *Letters to an Imaginary Friend* in 1962 and volume four in 1985?

A. Thomas McGrath.

Q. What shared fantasy world anthologies were edited by Emma Bull and Will Shetterly?

A. The *Liavek* books.

Q. James McGillivray, a newspaper reporter in the early 1900s, is credited with first making known the exploits of what mythical American hero?

A. Paul Bunyan.

Q. What Will Weaver novel chronicles the Indian–white struggle in Minnesota?

A. *Red Earth, White Earth* (1986).

———◆———

Q. Where was Anne French, one of America's most popular authors at the turn of the century, born in 1869?

A. St. Paul.

———◆———

Q. What do author J. F. Powers's initials stand for?

A. James Farl.

———◆———

Q. Where is Rebecca Hill's second novel, *Among Birches,* set?

A. A fictional town called Bracken, Minnesota.

———◆———

Q. What Carl Milles statue of an Indian stands in the St. Paul city hall?

A. The *Peace Memorial.*

———◆———

Q. Who wrote the 1988 Minnesota-based *Three Nights in the Heart of the Earth*?

A. Brett Laidlaw.

———◆———

Q. Who wrote *Boxelder Bug Variations* and *Going Home Crazy: An Alphabet of China Essays*?

A. Bill Holm (a member of the English department at Southwest State University in Marshall).

Q. How tall is author Frederick Manfred?

A. Six feet, nine inches.

———◆———

Q. According to legend, the Great Lakes were scooped out to provide drinking water for what mythological creature?

A. Paul Bunyan's giant blue ox, Babe.

———◆———

Q. What did author Tim O'Brien receive as a result of a shrapnel wound?

A. The Purple Heart.

———◆———

Q. What Minneapolis author of the science fiction mercenary novel *Not for Glory* often wears a Banana Republic vest?

A. Joel Rosenberg.

———◆———

Q. Where does author Jon Hassler teach?

A. St. John's University in Collegeville.

———◆———

Q. Who wrote the children's book *The Treasure on the Johnny Smoker*?

A. Minnesotan Mildred Houghton Comfort.

———◆———

Q. What did Robert Sherrill, author of *The Accidental President, a Biography of Lyndon Johnson,* title his Hubert Humphrey biography?

A. *The Drugstore Liberal.*

Q. What 1988 Anthony Schmitz novel was set in Minnesota?

A. *Lost Souls.*

---◆---

Q. At what two Minnesota schools did poet James Arlington Wright teach?

A. The University of Minnesota and Macalester College.

---◆---

Q. What Carol Bly story was reprinted in *The Best American Short Stories 1983*?

A. "The Dignity of Life."

---◆---

Q. Who told the story of a half-breed Sioux boy in *Good Thunder*?

A. John M. Solensten.

---◆---

Q. What poet/teacher/novelist/critic, who was one of the "Fugitives," taught at the University of Minnesota from 1951 to 1968?

A. Allen Tate.

---◆---

Q. What blind Minnesota author wrote *Homecoming* (1953)?

A. Borghild Dahl.

---◆---

Q. The Jon Hassler short story, "Anniversary," anthologized in *Blossoms & Blizzards*, first appeared in what publication?

A. *Redbook* magazine.

Q. Who was born Ramon Felipe San Juan Mario Silvo Enrico Alvarez del Rey on June 2, 1912, in Clydesdale?

A. Science fiction author and publisher Lester del Rey.

---◆---

Q. What does Kellogg artist Don Kreofsky create?

A. Carousel horses.

---◆---

Q. What southern Minnesota author wrote *Snowbird*, a 1980 ALA Best Book for Young Adults?

A. Patricia Calvert.

---◆---

Q. What role-playing game did University of Minnesota professor and author M.A.R. Barker create?

A. Empire of the Petal Throne.

---◆---

Q. What was the subject of Megan Terry's play *Keep Tightly Closed in a Cool, Dry Place*?

A. The Congdon murders.

---◆---

Q. What Edina poet wrote *Words with Wrinkled Knees* and *Cold Stars and Fireflies*, chosen by the Library of Congress as one of the one hundred best books of 1984?

A. Barbara Ebensen.

---◆---

Q. What seasonal poem was published in book form by Minnesotan Tom Hegg?

A. *A Cup of Christmas Tea.*

SPORTS & LEISURE

CHAPTER FIVE

Q. What coach of the 1980 Olympic hockey champions has also coached the St. Cloud State hockey team, the Gophers, and the North Stars?

A. Herb Brooks.

———◆———

Q. What sport put Michael J. Gibbons and Thomas J. Gibbons in the Minnesota Sports Hall of Fame?

A. Boxing.

———◆———

Q. What team that Max Berger bought for $15,000 in 1947 became the Minneapolis Lakers?

A. The Detroit Gems.

———◆———

Q. What Minneapolis resident won the 1988 North American Scrabble championship?

A. Bob Watson.

———◆———

Q. What did Stephany Nielsen, Miss Bloomington, say when she flubbed an *a cappella* half-time attempt of the national anthem?

A. "Aaaaw rats!" (1976).

Q. How many Minnesotans participated in organized softball in 1989?

A. One million.

—◆—

Q. What school, which has the only intercollegiate wheelchair basketball team in Minnesota, won intercollegiate titles in 1981, 1983, and 1986?

A. Southwest State University in Marshall.

—◆—

Q. Who holds the Viking career record for sacking the quarterback?

A. Carl Eller.

—◆—

Q. According to Minnesota mythology, what always occurs during the state high school basketball tournament?

A. A snowstorm.

—◆—

Q. What new NFL franchise was formed in Minneapolis in 1929?

A. The Redjackets.

—◆—

Q. Whom did the Twins beat four games to three in the 1987 World Series?

A. The St. Louis Cardinals.

—◆—

Q. What small college defeated the University of Chicago in football, 7 to 0, in 1916?

A. Carleton College.

Q. Where did Olga Korbut and Mary Lou Retton perform together for the first time, in November 1989?

A. The Met Center.

———◆———

Q. Where was Vern Mikkelson, Hamline basketball star and Minneapolis Laker, born?

A. Askov.

———◆———

Q. In 1990 what University of Minnesota graduate was traded from the Milwaukee Bucks to the Minnesota Timberwolves?

A. Randy Breuer.

———◆———

Q. What winner of the 1986 and 1989 Tour de France moved to Wayzata?

A. Greg LeMond.

———◆———

Q. When Dave Kingman hit a baseball 195 feet straight up into one of the eleven-inch holes in the Metrodome roof—and it stuck there—what did the umpires rule the play?

A. A ground rule double.

———◆———

Q. What did the Washington Senators become in 1961?

A. The Minnesota Twins.

———◆———

Q. Where was all-time great pacer Dan Patch bred?

A. Savage.

Q. How much did the Sony JumboTron color scoreboard in the Metrodome cost?

A. Five million dollars.

———◆———

Q. Who made the all-time high school hockey tournament record in 1951 with fifteen goals and three assists?

A. John Mayasich (the top five tournament scorers are from Eveleth).

———◆———

Q. What did Minnesota native Bronko Nagurski help the Chicago Bears achieve with his blocking in 1934?

A. The first perfect record in NFL history (13-0).

———◆———

Q. What all-pro athlete was traded to the Vikings in 1989?

A. Herschel Walker.

———◆———

Q. Who set the record for lifetime touchdown passes in 1975?

A. Fran Tarkenton.

———◆———

Q. What national champion drag racer came from Maple Grove?

A. Tom Hoover.

———◆———

Q. What Minnesota football personality sat on the Lakers' bench?

A. Bud Grant.

Q. What year is the International Special Olympics scheduled for the Twin Cities?

A. 1991.

———◆———

Q. What percentage of the six thousand participants in the Twin Cities Marathon come from Minnesota?

A. Sixty percent.

———◆———

Q. How many members of the 1956 Olympic hockey team were from Eveleth, Minnesota?

A. Four.

———◆———

Q. Where was the first recorded football game between women?

A. Gustavus Adolphus College (1923).

———◆———

Q. With Minnesota ranking number one in snowmobiles per capita, how many Minnesotans are there for every snowmobile?

A. Twenty.

———◆———

Q. George Mikan was one of the first four players to be elected into what?

A. The Basketball Hall of Fame.

———◆———

Q. For what was Gar Wood named to the Minnesota Sports Hall of Fame?

A. Speedboat racing.

Q. What former professional wrestler became a television producer and wrestling promoter?

A. Verne Gagne.

———◆———

Q. What St. Thomas graduate was the first Minnesotan to win Wimbledon?

A. Jeanne Arth.

———◆———

Q. Who was the only athlete recognized in curling in the Minnesota Sports Hall of Fame as of 1990?

A. Robert Dunbar (inducted in 1958).

———◆———

Q. What Minnesota marathoner, later injured in a farm accident, won the London Marathon in 1981?

A. Dick Beardsley.

———◆———

Q. Who made 3,129 points by March 17, 1980, unmatched by any other boy or girl in high school basketball?

A. Janet Karvonen.

———◆———

Q. From only three in the early fifties, the Twin Cities had how many hockey rinks in 1990?

A. Forty.

———◆———

Q. Who bought the Twins from Calvin Griffith?

A. Carl Pohlad.

Q. Who was the first commissioner of the ABA, headquartered in Minneapolis?

A. George Mikan.

———◆———

Q. Where is wrestler Jessie ("The Body") Ventura from?

A. Brooklyn Park.

———◆———

Q. What were the names of the teams in Gustavus Adolphus College's famous women's football game?

A. The Heavies and the Leans.

———◆———

Q. What type of skiing is done at the French Regional Park on Medicine Lake, Theodore Wirth Park, Hyland Park, Como Park, and Phalen Park?

A. Nighttime cross-country skiing on lighted trails.

———◆———

Q. What Twins pitcher fanned 206 in 1962 and 202 in 1963?

A. Camilio Pascual.

———◆———

Q. What track and field athlete was made a charter member of the Minnesota Sports Hall of Fame in 1958?

A. Fortune Gordien.

———◆———

Q. What disaster hit the Metropolitan Area Stadium less than two months before it was opened?

A. A fire.

Q. What Lutsen native—age twenty-eight at the 1984 Olympics—has been a member of the U.S. World Cup ski team since she was fifteen?

A. Cynthia Nelson.

———◆———

Q. What University of Minnesota hockey player was signed to the Rangers behind the locked door of a Pullman car?

A. Clarence ("Taffy") Abel.

———◆———

Q. When was University of Minnesota quarterback Sandy Stephens named to the All-American team?

A. 1961.

———◆———

Q. Who headed the commission that brought the 1992 Superbowl to the Metrodome?

A. Marilyn Carlson Nelson.

———◆———

Q. Who was the American League Rookie of the Year in 1964?

A. Tony Oliva.

———◆———

Q. For what establishment did the Road Warriors act as bouncers?

A. Gramma B's.

———◆———

Q. What Minnesotan was the first American to finish the Boston Marathon in 1972?

A. Bruce Mortenson.

Q. What Hamline graduate coached the first intercollegiate basketball game and established five-man basketball?

A. Raymond Kaighn.

———✦———

Q. How many snowmobile fatalities occurred in Minnesota in the 1987–88 winter?

A. Seventeen.

———✦———

Q. What former Vikings running back is now an actor in Los Angeles?

A. Ed Marinaro.

———✦———

Q. What part of Minnesota has the best brown trout streams and turkey habitat?

A. Southeastern.

———✦———

Q. What did Denny Yaider, a Twins fan from Rochester, do with Tiger Chet Lemon's home-run ball October 8, 1987?

A. Threw it back.

———✦———

Q. What do the Minnesota Monarchs play?

A. Volleyball.

———✦———

Q. For what two sports is John S. Johnson recognized in the Minnesota Sports Hall of Fame?

A. Speed skating and bicycle racing.

Q. Jim Pollard was the general manager of what ABA franchise, 1967–68?

A. The Minnesota Muskies.

———◆———

Q. In what sport did Osseo teenager Deborah Anderson win the national youth championship in 1985 and 1986 and the young adult championship in 1987?

A. Archery.

———◆———

Q. What northern Minnesotan was called perhaps the greatest college football player of all time by sportswriter Grantland Rice?

A. Bronko Nagurski.

———◆———

Q. What did Brennan and Scott Olson, brothers from Bloomington, invent in 1980?

A. Rollerblades.

———◆———

Q. Who batted .412 in the 1987 World Series?

A. Steve Lombardozzi.

———◆———

Q. St. Olaf beat Carleton 43–0 in what event on September 17, 1977?

A. The nation's first metric football game.

———◆———

Q. What is the roof of the Hubert H. Humphrey Metrodome coated with?

A. Teflon.

Q. What were the odds against the Twins' winning the World Series on February 18, 1987?

A. 150 to 1.

Q. What athletic endeavor is Walter Hoover cited for in the Minnesota Sports Hall of Fame?

A. Rowing.

Q. What percentage of Minnesotans sit in a boat or stand on the shore in an attempt to catch a walleye on opening day?

A. Twenty-five percent.

Q. What did 27,167 fans use to get in the *Guinness Book of World Records* during halftime of a Kicks' game on July 16, 1980?

A. Kazoos.

Q. What golf course is to host the U.S. Open Golf Tournament in 1991?

A. Hazeltine.

Q. What did Harmon Killebrew achieve on August 10, 1971?

A. His five hundredth career home run.

Q. Who was named Rookie of the Year in 1958 after joining the Minneapolis Lakers as a first-round draft pick?

A. Elgin Baylor.

Q. Who was Rookie of the Year for the American League in 1967?

A. Rod Carew.

———◆———

Q. What Edina resident set a record at the Twin Cities Marathon for the age-seventy-and-over women's class in 1987?

A. Helen Ruter (5:23:30).

———◆———

Q. Vern Mikkelsen was the manager of what 1968–69 ABA franchise?

A. The Minnesota Pipers.

———◆———

Q. What is written on Callum Devillier's tombstone in Lakewood Cemetery?

A. "World Champion Marathon Dancer, 3,780 Continuous Hours."

———◆———

Q. Who won the American League Cy Young Award in 1970?

A. Jim Perry.

———◆———

Q. How long does it take to convert the Metrodome from one sport to another?

A. About two hours.

———◆———

Q. Where is the Hockey Hall of Fame?

A. Eveleth.

Q. What Winona-born athlete won her first national title in swimming at fourteen?

A. Tracy Caulkins.

Q. What year did Harmon Killebrew hit forty-nine homers and Tony Oliva win both the batting title (.323) and most hits (217)?

A. 1964.

Q. In what sport did hockey's Johnny Mariucci first star at the University of Minnesota?

A. Football.

Q. What Minnesota boxer fought Jack Dempsey for the world crown in 1923?

A. Tommy Gibbons.

Q. What sport has former Minnesotan Dennis Breen taught Sylvester Stallone, Nick Cord, and Stephanie Powers?

A. Polo.

Q. When did Racine, Kenosha, and Minneapolis drop out of the NFL?

A. 1925.

Q. What did MADD stand for in Minnesota in the late 1970s?

A. Minnesotans Against the Downtown Dome.

Q. What coach has had more victories in college football than all but four other coaches?

A. John Gagliardi (St. John's University).

◆

Q. Hank Aaron and Willie Mays joined others in what event on July 13, 1965?

A. The only All-Star Game played at the Met.

◆

Q. In 1972, the basketball game between what two teams produced one of the most notorious fights in college basketball history?

A. Minnesota vs. Ohio State.

◆

Q. What figure skater was inducted into the Minnesota Sports Hall of Fame in 1963?

A. Robin Lee.

◆

Q. What wheelchair athlete came in first of the 4,572 finishers at the Twin Cities Marathon in 1988 with a time of 2:14:05?

A. Bob (Bart) Bardwell of Stewartville.

◆

Q. Who did Hank Stram of the Kansas City Chiefs claim "looked like a Chinese fire drill" at Super Bowl IV?

A. The Minnesota Vikings.

◆

Q. Who threw the first ball of the 1965 World Series?

A. Hubert Humphrey.

Q. What year did the Lakers move from Minneapolis to Los Angeles?

A. 1960.

———◆———

Q. What was the nickname of Frankie Brimsek of the Hockey Hall of Fame?

A. Mister Zero.

———◆———

Q. What active fox-hunting, boating, and English-style football club was established in Fairmont by English settlers?

A. The Fairmont Sportsmen.

———◆———

Q. Who threw the only nine-inning no-hitter at the Met?

A. Jack Kralick of the Twins (August 26, 1962).

———◆———

Q. Who was Minnesota's finest in the sport of harness racing?

A. George Loomis.

———◆———

Q. In what sport does St. John's University hold the all-time NCAA record for consecutive shutouts?

A. Soccer (thirteen consecutive shutouts).

———◆———

Q. What wrestling television show was produced in Minnesota?

A. "All-Star Wrestling."

Q. What was Bronko Nagurski's first name?

A. Branislaw.

———◆———

Q. In what type of racing did Thomas Milton of the Minnesota Sports Hall of Fame compete?

A. Auto racing.

———◆———

Q. Who played all nine positions in a Twins' win over the A's on September 22, 1968?

A. Cesar Tovar.

———◆———

Q. What coach of the 1956 U.S. Olympic hockey team played defense for the Chicago Black Hawks?

A. Johnny Mariucci.

———◆———

Q. What is the Wilderness Trek, held in Ely every February?

A. A cross-country ski race.

———◆———

Q. What Minnesota Sports Hall of Fame member announced the Dempsey–Gibbons fight?

A. Halsey Hall.

———◆———

Q. How many fans can the Metrodome seat for basketball?

A. 56,000.

Q. When did Duluth drop out of the NFL?

A. 1928.

———◆———

Q. How many abandoned railroad beds has the Department of Natural Resources converted into bike trails?

A. Eight.

———◆———

Q. In the 1981–82 season, how many former players did the University of Minnesota have in the NHL?

A. Sixteen.

———◆———

Q. Who did the Vikings beat 37–13 in their first game?

A. The Chicago Bears.

———◆———

Q. Who was the only Twin chosen for the 1987 All-Star Team?

A. Kirby Puckett.

———◆———

Q. What three states ranked above Minnesota in ducks shot in 1988?

A. California, Louisiana, and Texas.

———◆———

Q. Where did *Sports Illustrated* hold its 1987 World Series brunch?

A. The Minneapolis Institute of the Arts.

Q. How many penalty minutes did Swede Roland Erikson rack up in his first season with the North Stars?

A. Only ten.

Q. Where is the ball Dave Kingman hit up into the roof of the Metrodome, bringing a new ruling into the books?

A. The Baseball Hall of Fame in Cooperstown.

Q. What did the Denver Dynamos become in 1976?

A. The Minnesota Kicks.

Q. Hunting seasons for what animal have been held in Minnesota every other year since 1971?

A. Moose (there are about eight thousand in the state).

Q. What caused 17,697 fans to evacuate the Met on August 25, 1970?

A. A bomb scare.

Q. What cardboard boxes did a photo of the Twins decorate?

A. Wheaties.

Q. What six-foot, ten-inch star left Chicago to average 21.3 points a game for the Minneapolis Lakers in their first season?

A. George Mikan.

Q. What Minneapolis wrestler won worldwide acclaim as the Payne Avenue Derrick?

A. Otto Selin.

Q. How many parties per day are allowed on the Lake One chain near Ely in the Boundary Waters Canoe Area Wilderness?

A. Twenty-two (as of summer 1989).

Q. Where did Fran Tarkenton play between his two stints with the Vikings?

A. The New York Giants (1967).

Q. How many goals did Allan Willey score against the Cosmos in 1978 to set an NASL playoff record that lasted until 1980?

A. Five.

Q. For what do the Twins use the Gophers' locker room at the Metrodome?

A. A nursery for their children.

Q. What did the Vikings' Wally Hilgenberg warm in a sauna and smuggle onto the sidelines on December 4, 1977?

A. A fifteen-pound rock.

Q. What Minnesota Gopher was center on the 1949 All-American college football team?

A. Clayton Tonnemaker.

Q. What Minnesota Gopher was named to the 1977–78 All American basketball team?

A. Mychal Thompson.

———◆———

Q. How many ducks were shot by hunters in Minnesota in 1988?

A. 248,000.

———◆———

Q. What two places claim ballplayer Roger Maris?

A. Hibbing, Minnesota, and Fargo, North Dakota.

———◆———

Q. How much does the pitcher's mound at the Metrodome weigh?

A. 26,000 pounds.

———◆———

Q. How many deer hunting zones does Minnesota have?

A. Four.

———◆———

Q. What Viking was the NFL's top receiver in 1979?

A. Ahmad Rashad.

———◆———

Q. In what sport do Olympic medalists and fraternal twins Dennis and Duane Koslowski compete?

A. Greco-Roman wrestling.

Q. What St. Paul native had a long-time feud with George Steinbrenner?

A. Dave Winfield.

———◆———

Q. What place did five-time national champion Cynthia Nelson take in downhill skiing in the 1976 Olympics?

A. Bronze.

———◆———

Q. What year did Minnesota have the leading passer (Fran Tarkenton) and the leading rusher and scorer (Chuck Foreman)?

A. 1975.

———◆———

Q. Where does Grandma's Marathon, which ends in Duluth, begin?

A. Two Harbors.

———◆———

Q. How much did the Metrodome cost?

A. Fifty-five million dollars.

———◆———

Q. What season did the Minnesota North Stars become an NHL expansion team?

A. 1967–68.

———◆———

Q. Who hit grand-slam home runs to clinch games one and six for the Twins in the 1987 World Series?

A. Dan Gladden and Kent Hrbek.

Q. When did the Vikings re-acquire Fran Tarkenton?

A. 1972.

———◆———

Q. What did Paul Gerhardt want when he blocked the June 1955 ground breaking for the Metropolitan Area Stadium with his farm machinery?

A. $122,000.

———◆———

Q. What 1990 Kentucky Derby winner was owned by ninety-two-year-old Minnesotan Frances Genter?

A. Unbridled.

———◆———

Q. What Minnesota golfer won the first U.S. Women's Open in 1946?

A. Patty Berg.

———◆———

Q. What trophy, going back to the horse and wagon days, is the objective of the Michigan–Minnesota football game?

A. The Little Brown Jug.

———◆———

Q. What was the state muskellunge record as of early 1990?

A. Fifty-four pounds.

———◆———

Q. In what sport did Dorothy Franey Langkop excel?

A. Speed skating.

Q. Who pitched two innings for the Havana Sugar Kings in a postseason exhibition game against the Minneapolis Millers in 1960?

A. Fidel Castro.

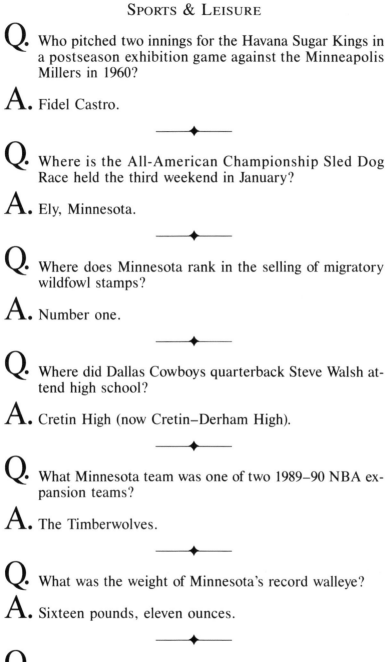

Q. Where is the All-American Championship Sled Dog Race held the third weekend in January?

A. Ely, Minnesota.

Q. Where does Minnesota rank in the selling of migratory wildfowl stamps?

A. Number one.

Q. Where did Dallas Cowboys quarterback Steve Walsh attend high school?

A. Cretin High (now Cretin–Derham High).

Q. What Minnesota team was one of two 1989–90 NBA expansion teams?

A. The Timberwolves.

Q. What was the weight of Minnesota's record walleye?

A. Sixteen pounds, eleven ounces.

Q. Who pinch-hit the 1991 World Series winning single?

A. Gene Larkin (with one out and bases loaded).

Q. Who beat former Russian chess champion Boris Gulko during a 1988 exhibition game when Gulko defeated thirty other players?

A. Fifteen-year-old Minnesotan Nathaniel Graham.

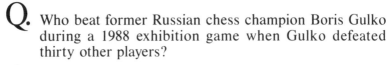

Q. Who was the winner of the 1981 Sullivan Award—at age fifteen the youngest winner ever—and the 1982 Sportswoman of the Year?

A. Tracy Caulkins.

Q. Who was the Women's Major Fast Pitch National Tournament batting champion in 1965?

A. Minnesotan Jan Berkland (.455).

Q. How many fans can the Metrodome seat for football?

A. 63,000.

Q. Which Smith, one of three in the National Football Foundation's Hall of Fame, was a 1941 Heisman Trophy winner?

A. Bruce ("Boo") Smith, Minnesota running back.

Q. How many career home runs did Harman Killebrew hit?

A. 573.

Q. What college basketball event is scheduled for the Twin Cities in 1992?

A. The NCAA Final Four.

Q. What University of Minnesota alumna made the only hole in one in the history of the U.S. Women's Open?

A. Patty Berg (1959).

———◆———

Q. When was the Metropolitan Area Stadium in Bloomington built?

A. 1956.

———◆———

Q. What coach brought the University of Minnesota to the Big Ten basketball championship in his first season?

A. Bill Musselman.

———◆———

Q. How far below the ground is the playing field at the Metrodome?

A. Fifty feet.

———◆———

Q. Who played in the first game at the Met?

A. Minneapolis and Wichita (American Association).

———◆———

Q. What two Duluth Eskimos were among the charter members of the Professional Football Hall of Fame?

A. Johnny Blood and Ernie Nevers.

———◆———

Q. How many years in a row did the Minnesota Gophers win the Big Ten in football, starting in 1934?

A. Five.

Q. In 1990, how much did it cost to rent one of the Viking's 115 private suites in the Metrodome for the entire year?

A. $47,000.

Q. What did Lewis Rober of the Minneapolis Fire Department initiate in 1895?

A. The first game of outdoor softball (for a time called kittenball).

Q. Who played at the Met for the first time with his New York Cosmos on June 9, 1976?

A. Pele.

Q. What bowler was the fourth woman to be named to the Minnesota Sports Hall of Fame?

A. Jean Havlish.

Q. Where did waterskiing originate in 1922?

A. Lake City (on Lake Pepin).

Q. Minnesota has provided more Olympic and professional athletes in what sport than any other state?

A. Hockey.

Q. Who batted only .191 in 1987, but had sixteen homers in fifty-five hits?

A. Tim Laudner.

Q. After leading Minnesota to the Big Ten basketball championship in 1954–55, who was named to the All-American team?

A. Dick Garmaker.

Q. What St. Paul native was hired as the youngest umpire in the American League?

A. Tim Tschida.

Q. Where was the U.S. Olympic Festival held in 1990?

A. The Twin Cities.

Q. Who was named to the Minnesota Sports Hall of Fame in rifle marksmanship in 1959?

A. Dr. Emmet Swanson.

Q. What year did the state of Minnesota introduce a lottery?

A. 1990.

Q. What is the name of Minnesota's parimutuel racetrack?

A. Canterbury Downs.

Q. What Viking was injured in a 1973 motorcycle accident that broke his back, arms, and one leg?

A. Karl Kassulke.

Q. What happened to the Hubert H. Humphrey Metrodome on November 18, 1981?

A. The roof deflated (because of a ten-inch snowfall).

———◆———

Q. How much do Minnesotans spend yearly fishing for walleyes?

A. Over $500 million.

———◆———

Q. Who did umpire Tim Tschida throw out of the game for having sandpaper and an emery board in his back pocket?

A. Twins pitcher Joe Niekro.

———◆———

Q. How many pounds of air per square foot keep the Metrodome inflated?

A. Six.

———◆———

Q. What Eveleth native was considered the best goaltender in the NHL in 1941?

A. Frankie Brimsek.

———◆———

Q. How many times has Jim Klobuchar climbed the Matterhorn?

A. Six.

———◆———

Q. What North Shore mail carrier has a five-hundred-mile sled dog race named after him?

A. John Beargrease.

Q. What 1980 Olympian signed on directly to the North Stars?

A. Steve Christoff.

◆

Q. In what sport besides football was Bronko Nagurski named to the Minnesota Sports Hall of Fame?

A. Wrestling.

◆

Q. What happened to George Mikan in game four, which did not stop him from leading the Lakers to victory over Washington postseason in 1948–49?

A. He broke his wrist.

◆

Q. Minnesota artist Bud Chapman, painter of "18 Infamous Golf Holes," carries what handicap?

A. One.

◆

Q. When did the Minneapolis Redjackets drop out of the NFL?

A. 1931.

◆

Q. What town is home to six Olympic hockey players and the Christian Brothers Hockey Stick Factory?

A. Warroad.

◆

Q. When was the first opening day for the Minnesota Twins?

A. Friday, April 21, 1961.

Q. How much does it cost per hour to heat or air condition the Metrodome?

A. A thousand dollars.

———◆———

Q. What handball player made the Minnesota Sports Hall of Fame in 1963?

A. George Quam.

———◆———

Q. In what sport did the Minnesota Grizzlies participate?

A. Professional wrestling.

———◆———

Q. Who was the first Twins player to bat in their first World Series appearance in 1965?

A. Zoilo Versalles.

———◆———

Q. What born-again former Prince bodyguard competed as "Mountain Man" in professional wrestling?

A. Big Chick.

———◆———

Q. What all-star pitcher did the Twins trade in 1989?

A. Frank Viola.

———◆———

Q. What event involves bathtubs, large dip nets, washtubs, and the light of the moon?

A. The smelt run on the north shore of Lake Superior.

SCIENCE & NATURE

CHAPTER SIX

Q. Who performed the world's first successful open-heart surgery on a five-year-old named Jackie Johnson in 1952?

A. F. John Lewis and C. Walton Lillehei (the University of Minnesota Hospital).

◆

Q. What political figure received a hearing aid from Starkey Laboratories in the Twin Cities?

A. Ronald Reagan.

◆

Q. What is the Minnesota state mushroom?

A. The morel.

◆

Q. What are the only existing remains of Arctic explorer Roald Amundson, which are now preserved at Concordia College at Moorhead?

A. Two teeth that were extracted when he was at the college to speak.

◆

Q. What does MMPI stand for?

A. Minnesota Multiphasic Personality Inventory (the world's most popular personality test).

Q. What did Frederick Nussbaum begin building in 1913?

A. The Como Park Observatory.

———◆———

Q. How many acres of virgin forest were there in Minnesota when the first white settlers arrived?

A. 31,500,000.

———◆———

Q. For what was Minneapolis architect Leroy S. Buffington granted a patent in 1888, although he later sued builders when it was not enforced?

A. "Iron Building Construction" (the first skyscraper plans).

———◆———

Q. Where were 33,588 hawks sighted on September 15, 1978?

A. Hawk Ridge near Duluth (considered the best place to watch hawks in North America).

———◆———

Q. Where was the first American memorial to Alfred Nobel built in 1963?

A. Gustavus Adolphus College (the Alfred Nobel Hall of Science).

———◆———

Q. Who came to Minneapolis from Australia in 1940 to treat polio victims?

A. Sister Elizabeth Kenny.

———◆———

Q. Who built Grand Mound?

A. The Laurel Indians (200 B.C. to A.D. 800 or later).

Q. Beginning in July 1990, what are the requirements for packaging of products sold in Minneapolis?

A. Returnable, recyclable, or degradable.

———◆———

Q. What disease is treated by the Minnesota Model?

A. Alcoholism.

———◆———

Q. Where is Dr. Albert Kuhfeld the curator of instruments?

A. The Bakken Library of Electricity in Life (on the west shore of Lake Calhoun).

———◆———

Q. What three vegetables for the canning industry is Minnesota the leading producer of?

A. Sweet corn, peas, and beans.

———◆———

Q. What is the Minnesota state bird?

A. The common loon.

———◆———

Q. Who led expeditions to the north and south poles?

A. Will Steger.

———◆———

Q. How many people were victims of tornadoes between 1900 and 1982 in Minnesota?

A. 103.

Q. What doctor, who had learned surgery at the University of Minnesota, performed the world's first heart transplant in 1967?

A. Christiaan Barnard (in South Africa).

———◆———

Q. In 1990, what group of people had the longest life expectancy in the world?

A. Minnesota women (79.8 years).

———◆———

Q. What is unusual about Edinborough Park in Edina?

A. It is indoors.

———◆———

Q. What University of Minnesota engineering graduate, who developed the first wearable pacemaker in 1958 with C. Walton Lillehei, founded Medtronics, Inc.?

A. Earl Bakken.

———◆———

Q. Why did movies, churches, and other places that attracted crowds close in November 1918?

A. An influenza epidemic struck the Twin Cities.

———◆———

Q. What flower is it illegal to pick in Minnesota?

A. A lady's-slipper.

———◆———

Q. How many prehistoric carvings comprise the Jeffers Petroglyphs?

A. More than two thousand.

Q. What University of Minnesota alumnus built the first supercomputer?

A. Seymour Cray.

———◆———

Q. How many mosquitoes can Minnesota's most common bat, the brown bat, eat in an hour?

A. Five hundred.

———◆———

Q. How long does it take the Aerial Lift Bridge in Duluth to raise to its complete height of 138 feet?

A. Fifty-five seconds.

———◆———

Q. What type of bird was thought to be extinct until it was found wintering at Silver Lake in Rochester?

A. The giant Canada goose.

———◆———

Q. Who was the first woman to reach the North Pole on foot?

A. Minnesotan Ann Bancroft.

———◆———

Q. Where is the world's busiest transplant center?

A. The University of Minnesota.

———◆———

Q. For what was first lady Barbara Bush treated at the Mayo Clinic in 1990?

A. A thyroid condition.

Q. How many inches of snow do the Twin Cities average annually?

A. Forty-two.

—◆—

Q. What is the largest cave in the Midwest, discovered near Harmony by a farmer searching for lost pigs?

A. Niagara Cave.

—◆—

Q. Wendelin Grimm developed a hardy variety of what crop?

A. Alfalfa.

—◆—

Q. On Minnesota's state seal, what two items represent the state's natural features?

A. A waterfall and a forest (an Indian and a farmer symbolize the state's people).

—◆—

Q. Where does Minnesota's summer precipitation come from?

A. The tropical part of the Atlantic and the Gulf of Mexico.

—◆—

Q. What prehistoric rodent, up to nine feet long and weighing five hundred pounds, inhabited Minnesota?

A. Giant beavers (about the size of a black bear).

—◆—

Q. What percentage of Minnesota's original wetlands have been drained for agricultural purposes since the state was settled?

A. More than sixty percent.

Q. What essential modern need is Minnesota unable to supply for itself?

A. Energy.

———◆———

Q. More than a billion gross tons of earth were extracted from the Hull-Rust-Mahoning Mine, more than what other engineering marvel?

A. The Panama Canal.

———◆———

Q. What was the most popular display at the amusement park Wonderland (1905–12)?

A. The Infant House (with premature babies in incubators).

———◆———

Q. What college bestows an honorary doctorate on every Nobel laureate who comes to the campus?

A. Gustavus Adolphus.

———◆———

Q. What is the record high temperature in Minnesota?

A. 114.5 degrees (July 29, 1917, in Beardsley).

———◆———

Q. What executive officer of the Minnesota State Board of Health worked with Louis Pasteur in discovering the cure for rabies?

A. Charles Nathaniel Hewitt.

———◆———

Q. How many Indian burial mounds have been found in Minnesota?

A. More than ten thousand.

Q. What causes compasses on ships to be unreliable in Lake Superior's western basin?

A. Iron ore deposits on the lake bottom.

———◆———

Q. Where is the only typha operation in the United States that uses the fiber from cattails in stuffing, upholstery, and insulation?

A. Holt (Ness Typha Co.)

———◆———

Q. What is Minnesota's Emmy-winning PBS science series?

A. "Newton's Apple."

———◆———

Q. What Minnesota company developed the first implantable pacemakers?

A. Medtronics.

———◆———

Q. What innovation did Marvin Windows of Warroad, Minnesota, come up with in 1989?

A. Ninety-degree-angle, bent-glass windows.

———◆———

Q. Where was the first fully accredited school of nursing?

A. Rochester.

———◆———

Q. What percentage of taxpayers checked the Minnesota Nongame Wildlife Program donation on their tax forms in 1987?

A. Eight (number one of the thirty-four states that offered such a wildlife conservation program).

Q. Why were there no chickens at the Minnesota State Fair in 1985?

A. The avian flu was going around.

———◆———

Q. Although parts of southwestern Minnesota get less than forty inches of snow per year, how much does the northeastern part receive?

A. Seventy inches.

———◆———

Q. What Minnesota brewery brewed Billy Beer?

A. Cold Spring Brewing Company (Cold Spring).

———◆———

Q. What percentage of Minnesota land was originally covered with pine, spruce, and fir forests?

A. About forty percent.

———◆———

Q. What is the official state fish?

A. The walleye.

———◆———

Q. A canning plant in what Minnesota city originated and patented the equipment used in canning whole kernel corn?

A. Ortonville.

———◆———

Q. What is the occupation of Dr. John Najarian?

A. Chief of surgery at the University of Minnesota.

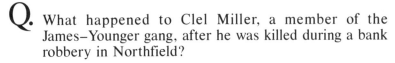

Q. What happened to Clel Miller, a member of the James–Younger gang, after he was killed during a bank robbery in Northfield?

A. He was dissected by medical students.

———◆———

Q. What does a loon have under each eye that allows it to adapt to fresh or salt water living?

A. A salt gland.

———◆———

Q. How old are the oldest manmade tools found in Minnesota?

A. About ten thousand years.

———◆———

Q. What are Minnesota's only two types of poisonous snakes?

A. The timber rattlesnake and the Massasauga or Pygmy rattlesnake.

———◆———

Q. What unusual one-acre field was planted at Bass Lake near Merrifield, Minnesota, in 1950?

A. It was the first cultivated wild rice field.

———◆———

Q. Where were Okabena apples developed?

A. Worthington.

———◆———

Q. Who began his medical career at age nine, standing on a box to administer ether while his father operated?

A. Charles Mayo.

Q. What is the soft red stone of Pipestone National Monument?

A. Catlinite.

—◆—

Q. How many days with at least one inch of snow cover does northeastern Minnesota get?

A. At least 140 days.

—◆—

Q. What is Minnesota's most productive bedrock aquifer, producing five hundred to one thousand gallons a minute from deep wells?

A. The Prairie du Chien-Jordan aquifer.

—◆—

Q. Between the years of 1870 to 1877, what plagued Minnesota farmers?

A. Grasshoppers.

—◆—

Q. How much of the iron ore produced during World War II came from the now inactive Hull-Rust-Mahoney Mine?

A. One-third.

—◆—

Q. How long is the waterfall located 150 feet underground in Niagara Cave?

A. Sixty feet.

—◆—

Q. What percentage of Minnesota land was originally covered by deciduous (not evergreen) forests?

A. Twenty-five percent.

Q. St. Thomas College graduate Dr. James Jude was one of three physicians to perfect what lifesaving technique?

A. CPR.

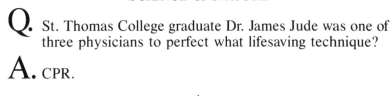

Q. Minnesota produces one of every six of what poultry product sold in the United States?

A. Turkeys.

Q. What is the most common nesting species of ducks in the state?

A. Mallards.

Q. Where was the record for loading iron ore set?

A. Two Harbors (twelve thousand tons in sixteen minutes).

Q. Where does Minnesota rank among the states in the number of timber wolves?

A. Second (after Alaska).

Q. Of the original 23,000,000 acres of wet and dry grasslands, Minnesotans plowed under all but how many?

A. Seventy-six thousand.

Q. Other than foot traffic, what are the only means of transportation allowed in the Superior-Quetico Primitive Region?

A. Canoe and hydroplane.

Q. What 3M invention started as a way to keep bookmarks in hymnals?

A. Post-it Notes.

Q. Who wrote *Rejuvenation: A Wellness Guide for Men and Women?*

A. Horst Rechelbacher.

Q. When was the world's first blood bank established at the Mayo Clinic?

A. 1933.

Q. What is Minnesota's record low temperature?

A. Fifty-nine degrees below zero (February 9, 1899, at the Leech Lake Dam, now Federal Dam).

Q. Who performed Minnesota's first heart-lung transplant in 1986 and the Midwest's first double-lung transplant in 1988?

A. Dr. Stuart Jamieson of the University of Minnesota Hospital.

Q. Edmond L. Croix of Dundas created what machine to remove the chaff from wheat during the milling process?

A. The Midlings Purifier.

Q. What University of Minnesota alumnus became an astronaut?

A. Donald ("Deke") Slayton.

Q. Where was the world's first successful bone marrow transplant performed in 1968?

A. The University of Minnesota (Doctors Robert Good and Richard Hong).

———◆———

Q. How many different calls does a loon have?

A. Four (wail, tremolo, yodel, and hoot).

———◆———

Q. What fraction of Minnesota's annual precipitation is received during the growing season?

A. About two-thirds.

———◆———

Q. What is cured in caves along the Straight River near Faribault?

A. Blue cheese.

———◆———

Q. What kinds of trees cover nearly one-fifth of Minnesota's total land area now?

A. Aspen and birch.

———◆———

Q. Who developed a suction device to prevent post-operative intestinal bleeding in 1945?

A. Dr. Owen H. Wangensteen, head of the department of surgery, at the University of Minnesota.

———◆———

Q. What is the largest open-pit iron ore mine in the world?

A. The Hull-Rust-Mahoning Mine (near Hibbing).

Q. What is the rugged northeastern region of Minnesota least affected by glacial action known as?

A. The Superior Uplands.

———◆———

Q. Where does Minnesota rank in number of hearing aid companies?

A. Number one.

———◆———

Q. What was the nickname of Wallace D. Armstrong, head of the department of biochemistry at the University of Minnesota?

A. Dr. Fluoridation.

———◆———

Q. What did William H. Jensen hide, neglecting to reveal its location before his death in 1960?

A. The skeleton of Browns Valley Man.

———◆———

Q. In 1905, the peak year, how many board feet of lumber were cut in Minnesota?

A. More than two billion.

———◆———

Q. Where was the first post-operative recovery room in a hospital established?

A. The Mayo Clinic.

———◆———

Q. What health care products company did hair designer Horst Rechelbacher found?

A. Aveda Corporation.

Q. What caused most of Minnesota's lakes?

A. Glaciation.

———◆———

Q. What University of Minnesota professor of surgery and biomedical engineering developed the first implantable insulin pump?

A. Henry Buchwald.

———◆———

Q. Alfred H. Hill and Theodore Lewis found almost eight thousand of what objects in Minnesota before 1895?

A. Indian mounds.

———◆———

Q. What is the earth's oldest living bird species, dating back sixty million years?

A. The common loon.

———◆———

Q. What is the common name of *cypripedium reginae*?

A. The showy lady's-slipper.

———◆———

Q. What was the second municipal rose garden planted in the United States?

A. The Lyndale Park Rose Garden (Lake Harriet).

———◆———

Q. What was the name of the huge prehistoric lake that shrank to become Lake Superior?

A. Duluth Lake.

Q. What Minnesota-based group pioneered the treatment of alcoholism as a disease?

A. The Hazelden Foundation, Center City.

◆

Q. How much tailings does manufacturing a ton of taconite pellets produce?

A. At least two tons.

◆

Q. What is the name given to the skeleton of a young woman found under nine feet of glacial silt near Pelican Rapids?

A. Minnesota Man.

◆

Q. Where is Lori Schmidt the dominant pack member?

A. The International Wolf Center (near Ely).

◆

Q. What does "3M" stand for?

A. Minnesota Mining and Manufacturing.

◆

Q. What new type of health care system was first used in Minnesota?

A. The HMO.

◆

Q. What is the area in southeastern Minnesota that was never touched by the four glaciers called?

A. The driftless area.

Q. What product, much maligned by GIs in World War II, was developed by Ancel Keys, director of the University of Minnesota's Laboratory of Physiological Hygiene?

A. K rations.

———◆———

Q. What is the Minnesota state tree?

A. The Norway pine or red pine.

———◆———

Q. Who began using the Carbon-14 isotope in 1945 to investigate photosynthesis?

A. Minnesotan Melvin Calvin.

———◆———

Q. What were three hundred miners working on the northeast side of Lake Vermilion looking for in 1865 and 1866?

A. Gold (none was ever found).

———◆———

Q. How many Minnesotans are employed in manufacturing?

A. More than 100,000.

———◆———

Q. How many duck species nest in Minnesota?

A. Nineteen.

———◆———

Q. Where are there more than two thousand roses in more than two hundred varieties?

A. The Rohrer Rose Garden, Winona.

Q. Where did Arctic and Antarctic explorer Will Steger go to college?

A. St. Thomas.

———◆———

Q. What did Russell Johnson, a professor in the department of microbiology at the University of Minnesota, develop and patent in 1988?

A. A vaccine for Lyme disease.

———◆———

Q. In one hundred years (1837–1937), enough homes were built from Minnesota lumber to provide how many houses for each Minnesota resident today?

A. Five (68 billion board feet).

———◆———

Q. Where are the Minnesota state hatcheries headquartered?

A. Glenwood.

———◆———

Q. What new product did 3M introduce in 1928?

A. Scotch tape.

———◆———

Q. Where is the series of north-south valleys and ridges that mark the western edge of the Keewatin Glacier?

A. Worthington.

———◆———

Q. Where are fossil snails, clams and oysters, coiled cephalopods, and shark teeth from the Cretaceous Period to be found?

A. The western Mesabi Range.

Q. Where did experiments using a human centrifuge lead to the development of the G suit and the BLB mask, used in high altitude flight?

A. The Mayo Clinic.

———◆———

Q. Who developed the first home thermostats in 1885?

A. Minneapolis Honeywell.

———◆———

Q. What is 3 miles long, 2 miles wide, and 535 feet deep, covering 1,600 acres?

A. The Hull-Rust-Mahoning Mine.

———◆———

Q. Where does Minnesota rank among the states for nesting bald eagles?

A. Second (Alaska is number one).

———◆———

Q. What did homesteaders at Lake Bemidji mistake for diamonds?

A. Quartzite.

———◆———

Q. What is the process of concentrating the iron of low grade ores called?

A. Beneficiating.

———◆———

Q. What 1871 law encouraged planting trees on the prairies?

A. The Tree Bounty Law.

Q. What is the area in southwestern Minnesota, where glaciers left deep deposits of soil-forming clay, sand, and gravel?

A. Dissected Till Plains.

———◆———

Q. In 1973, the Mayo Clinic was the first medical center in the country to use what type of scanning?

A. CT scanning.

———◆———

Q. In 1990, it was estimated that up to two hundred Minnesota lakes were adversely affected by what environmental problem?

A. Acid rain.

———◆———

Q. What prize did Doctors Philip Hench and Edward Kendall of the Mayo Clinic share with a Swiss doctor in 1950?

A. The Nobel Prize in medicine (for the effect of ACTH and cortisone).

———◆———

Q. What Minnesota county leads in wild rice production?

A. Aitkin County.

———◆———

Q. Where did Reserve Mining Company discharge its taconite tailings until 1980?

A. Directly into Lake Superior.

———◆———

Q. What was the first mine to use electricity in its operations?

A. The Hill-Annex Mine (Calumet).

Q. What company was Hamline graduate William Keye a co-founder of?

A. Control Data Corporation.

———◆———

Q. Where is Minnesota's largest prehistoric Indian burial mounds?

A. Grand Mound Interpretive Center, near International Falls.

———◆———

Q. What flotilla of canoes and small boats runs from Bemidji to Bellevue, cleaning garbage from the Mississippi River and its banks?

A. The Mississippi River Revival (MRR).

———◆———

Q. Who was the first person to occupy the American Legion Memorial Heart Research Professorship of Pediatrics and Medicine in Minnesota in 1950?

A. Lewis Thomas.

———◆———

Q. How many walleye fry are there to the ounce?

A. More than five thousand.

———◆———

Q. What relative of coal has its largest U.S. deposits in Minnesota?

A. Peat.

———◆———

Q. What is Hamline graduate Dr. Robert M. Page known as?

A. The "father of radar."

Q. What deer that inhabits Minnesota is the largest of seventeen known subspecies of whitetail deer in the nation?

A. The northern woodland whitetail.

———◆———

Q. How old are the rocks in the Boundary Waters Canoe Area?

A. Three billion years.

———◆———

Q. What rise in southwestern Minnesota prevented expansion of the glaciers?

A. Coteau des Prairies.

———◆———

Q. If Minnesota's groundwater was brought to the surface, how deep would it cover the whole state with fresh water?

A. Ten feet.

———◆———

Q. What performer who enchants audiences at the Como Park Zoo never eats red meat?

A. Sparky the Seal.

———◆———

Q. In ten years, what provided the equivalent of 3.5 million days of labor fighting forest fires in Minnesota and building thirty-five new state parks?

A. The Civilian Conservation Corps (CCC).

———◆———

Q. Peter Gideon developed what hardy northern apple?

A. The wealthy.

Q. What is the average winter low temperature in Minneapolis and St. Paul?

A. Four degrees.

———◆———

Q. What innovation did the James Ford Bell Museum introduce for children?

A. Major hands-on exhibits (The Touch and See Room).

———◆———

Q. What is the lifespan of the lady's-slipper, the state flower?

A. One hundred years.

———◆———

Q. What did a ride on Twin Cities streetcars and trolleys cost in the early 1900s?

A. One nickel.

———◆———

Q. What popular hot cereal was developed in Minnesota?

A. Cream of Wheat.

———◆———

Q. Big Mouth and Little Girl, who resided at the Minnesota Zoo, were what type of cetaceans?

A. Beluga whales.

———◆———

Q. What carved out the Minnesota River Valley?

A. The prehistoric Warren River, flowing from Lake Agassiz.

Q. Hamline graduate Dr. Richard Schwoebel was the in-flight director for what first Atlantic Ocean crossing?

A. A manned balloon.

———◆———

Q. Wheat from what country improved Minnesota's flour industry?

A. Russia.

———◆———

Q. The *Virginia* was the first of what type of transport to enter Minnesota via the Mississippi in 1823?

A. Steamboat.

———◆———

Q. What did Dr. Richard DeWall, physician-scientist in the University of Minnesota's department of surgery, develop in 1955?

A. The first successful heart-lung machine.

———◆———

Q. Where is the world's largest continuous batch washer, handling eight million pounds of laundry each year?

A. Rochester (TextileCareServicesDivision).

———◆———

Q. What was Minnesota's first skyscraper?

A. The Foshay Tower.

———◆———

Q. What was the Split Rock Lighthouse built to warn against?

A. The reefs in Beaver Bay (in Lake Superior).

Q. What percentage of the state's rural population uses groundwater sources for drinking?

A. Eighty-five percent.

———◆———

Q. In 1971, Minnesota had 89,000 breeding pairs of what type of fowl, higher than any other state?

A. Ducks.

———◆———

Q. What did Andrew G. Anderson and Carl Eric Wickham start in Hibbing with one old Hupmobile?

A. The Greyhound bus system.

———◆———

Q. Kato, sturdy, and proto are varieties of what vegetation developed by the University of Minnesota in 1989?

A. Soybeans.

———◆———

Q. How many dairy cows per square mile does Carver County have?

A. Sixty.

———◆———

Q. What is the earliest date of the Jeffers Petroglyphs in Cottonwood County?

A. 3,000 B.C.

———◆———

Q. What natural disaster decimated the Fairmont region in June 1873?

A. Rocky Mountain locusts.

Q. What are the limbs and branches left after logging called?

A. Slash.

———◆———

Q. What was one of the first packaged mixes, developed by General Mills in Minneapolis?

A. Bisquick.

———◆———

Q. What is *gavia immer* better known as?

A. The great northern diver or common loon.

———◆———

Q. What low-grade ore was mined after the richer iron ore was depleted?

A. Taconite.

———◆———

Q. How much higher is the Coteau des Prairies than the surrounding land?

A. About eight hundred feet.

———◆———

Q. In order to grow, what vegetation requires low-sulphate fresh water three to four feet deep on an organic lake bottom?

A. Wild rice.

———◆———

Q. St. Olaf College graduate Dr. Olaf Skinsnes is an international authority on what disease?

A. Leprosy.

SCIENCE & NATURE

Q. Loess soil, found in southeastern Minnesota, is laid down by what force?

A. Wind.

———◆———

Q. What area is known for its peony farms?

A. Faribault.

———◆———

Q. How many pounds of garbage do Minnesotans create every year?

A. 6.5 billion.

———◆———

Q. Mankato, St. Cloud, and Northfield formed the corners of what forest area?

A. The Big Woods.

———◆———

Q. In 1931, what natural disaster hit the Empire Builder train near Moorhead, lifting five seventy-ton cars and tossing one eighty feet into a ditch?

A. A tornado.

———◆———

Q. What famous physician practiced medicine in Le Sueur from 1858 to 1863?

A. William Worrell Mayo.

———◆———

Q. The St. Croix Valley—wide, U-shaped, with steep sides and a flat bottom—is a remnant of what?

A. An Ice Age river.

Q. Why did Laura Ingalls Wilder's family live in a dugout beside Plum Creek near Walnut Grove in the late 1800s?

A. For protection against harsh winter winds and prairie grass fires.

◆

Q. Where does Minnesota's winter precipitation originate?

A. The Pacific Ocean.

◆

Q. To what temperature is the iron-bearing rock of the Mesabi heated before cold water is sprayed on it?

A. More than four thousand degrees.

◆

Q. William Worrell Mayo was one of the first doctors to use what instrument to diagnose disease?

A. A microscope.

◆

Q. How many pounds of agrichemicals enter the environment in Minnesota each year?

A. Forty million pounds.

◆

Q. Who first successfully replaced a heart valve with an artificial valve?

A. C. Walton Lillehei (1958).

◆

Q. Voyageurs National Park is the last sanctuary in the continental United States for what animal?

A. The eastern timber wolf.

Q. When was beneficiating, which gave new life to the Iron Range, commercially activated?

A. 1955.

Q. What is the Minnesota state grain?

A. Wild rice.

Q. Who performed the world's first successful pancreas transplant in 1967?

A. Richard Lillehei and William Kelly.

Q. Where is Minnesota's largest deer park, with nearly one hundred tame deer?

A. Fort Detroit (Detroit Lakes).

Q. Six tons of what root were brought to Faribault for export in one week of 1859?

A. Ginseng.

Q. Two thousand hypodermically thin needles, spaced about five inches apart, simulate what at the University of Minnesota?

A. Rain.

Q. What prestigious quality award did IBM Rochester win in 1990?

A. The Malcolm Baldridge award.